"In *Authentic Excellence for Organizations*, the authors provide a roadmap for organizations to shift from 'Or' to '&' cultures, whereby the focus shifts from tension reduction to tension management, and both sides of singular organizational dynamics are honored, creating a more optimizing, values-centered culture. Flourishing organizations will adopt this transformative thinking!"

Dr. Rob Burrus, Dean, Cameron School of Business, University of North Carolina Wilmington

"This outstanding book by gifted leaders identifies 8 Essential &'s and their transformative optimizers for organizational flourishing. The fundamental premise behind the frameworks is that it takes practice and work. The authors describe a process that details how organizational members can harness their team's natural wisdom to flourish through the relentless pace and pressure of today's world. This will be required reading of my administrative team as it will assist leaders in developing teams through inclusive and values-centered culture rather than a fear-based culture."

Dr. Frederick Whitt, President, Lenoir Rhyne University

"*Authentic Excellence for Organizations* is a game changer. This book can help your organization achieve levels of excellence you never considered attainable. The authors present a clear and practical roadmap to achieve organizational flourishing."

Aidan Heaney, Head Coach, Men's Soccer, University of North Carolina Wilmington

"*Authentic Excellence for Organizations* examines a topic that is simple AND complex. I really enjoyed the vignettes at the beginning of each chapter, and the roadmaps provided for the 8 Essential '&'s' present a framework for helping any organization pursue authentic excellence."

Dr. Joseph Pino, Senior Vice President of Medical Education Novant Health and Executive Director of Southeast Area Health Education Center, and Associate Dean and Director of University of North Carolina School of Medicine Wilmington Campus, University of North Carolina at Chapel Hill

"The disruptive impact of the pandemic has forever changed the workplace. *Authentic Excellence for Organizations* is one of the most powerful new leadership books that I have read. It is a must-read. Opening chapter vignettes and the roadmaps provided for the 8 Essential '&'s' are powerful tools for any organization seeking to effectively move their organization 'to where the hockey puck is going' to achieve success in today's workplace."

Larry Clark, *Chancellor, Louisiana State University Shreveport*

"Too many times, leaders are limited by their ability to think only in dichotomies. This book demonstrates that leadership must be values-based and expansive; otherwise, fear-based need and power create a toxic culture that prevents giving voice to the complexities of organizational systems. Shifting from an 'Or' culture to '&' culture is hard work. The authors have adapted the Giving Voice to Values model to analyze, apply, and practice embracing essential organizational '&' values."

Dr. Lori Messinger, *Dean, College of Social Work, University of Tennessee*

AUTHENTIC EXCELLENCE FOR ORGANIZATIONS

Authentic Excellence for Organizations explores organizational culture from a values-based perspective and applies the psychological principles of values-based flourishing to organizations. Integrating the principles of Giving Voice to Values (GVV) and Authentic Excellence (AX), this book provides a process that details how organizations can harness their team's inherent wisdom to flourish through the relentless pace and pressure of today's world.

Moving beyond team-building strategies and programming, this book helps develop confidence in managing the tensions inherent in organizations. It explores:

- The difference between moral values and personal values;
- How both can be effectively expressed and managed in organizations;
- The possibilities of shifting from a fear-based culture of "Or" to an inclusive and values-centered culture of "&"; and
- How to practically create flourishing "&" cultures using the GVV model. How to create an organizational culture that effectively sustains "&s" like competitive & collaborative, productive & fulfilled, and innovation & tradition.

This book is intended for organizational leaders, members, and HR managers looking to develop strong and thriving teams. It also aligns with required or recommended reading for secondary or undergraduate courses that explore values, leadership, organizational development and performance, decision-making, ethics, and entrepreneurship.

R. Kelly Crace, PhD, is the Associate Vice President for Health & Wellness at William & Mary and Director of the Center for Mindfulness and Authentic Excellence (CMAX). He is a licensed psychologist and the co-author of *Authentic Excellence: Flourishing & Resilience in a Relentless World* and the *Life Values Inventory*.

Charles J. Hardy, PhD, is a Professor in the School of Health and Applied Human Sciences at the University of North Carolina Wilmington (UNCW). He served as the Founding Dean of the College of Health and Human Services (CHHS) at UNCW and the Jiann-Ping Hsu College of Public Health (JPHCOPH) at Georgia Southern University.

Robert L. Crace, MFA, is the Executive Director of the nonprofit Life Values Inventory Online, Inc. He is the co-author of *Authentic Excellence: Flourishing & Resilience in a Relentless World.* He is a Visiting Professor in Creative Writing & Literature at Stony Brook University.

GIVING VOICE TO VALUES

Series Editor: Mary C. Gentile

The *Giving Voice to Values* series is a collection of books on Business Ethics and Corporate Social Responsibility that brings a practical, solutions-oriented, skill-building approach to the salient questions of values-driven leadership.

Giving Voice to Values (GVV: www.GivingVoiceToValues.org) – the curriculum, the pedagogy and the research upon which it is based – was designed to transform the foundational assumptions upon which the teaching of business ethics is based, and importantly, to equip future business leaders to know not only what is right – but how to make it happen.

Giving Voice to Values
An Innovation and Impact Agenda
Jerry Goodstein and Mary C. Gentile

Collaborating for Climate Resilience
Ann Goodman and Nilda M. Mesa

Tactics for Racial Justice
Building an Antiracist Organization and Community
Shannon Joyce Prince

The Lawyer's Guide to Business Ethics
Keith William Diener

Authentic Excellence for Organizations
Creating Flourishing "&" Cultures
R. Kelly Crace, Charles J. Hardy, and Robert L. Crace

For more information about this series, please visit: www.routledge.com/Giving-Voice-to-Values/book-series/GVV

AUTHENTIC EXCELLENCE FOR ORGANIZATIONS

Creating Flourishing "&" Cultures

R. Kelly Crace, Charles J. Hardy,
and Robert L. Crace

Routledge
Taylor & Francis Group

LONDON AND NEW YORK

Graphic illustration and cover design by Keith Johnson

First published 2023
by Routledge
4 Park Square, Milton Park, Abingdon, Oxon OX14 4RN

and by Routledge
605 Third Avenue, New York, NY 10158

Routledge is an imprint of the Taylor & Francis Group, an informa business

British Library Cataloguing-in-Publication Data
A catalogue record for this book is available from the British Library

Library of Congress Cataloging-in-Publication Data
Names: Crace, R. Kelly, author. | Hardy, Charles J. (College teacher), author. | Crace, Robert L., author.
Title: Authentic excellence for organizations : creating flourishing "&" cultures / R. Kelly Crace, Charles J. Hardy and Robert L. Crace.
Description: Abingdon, Oxon ; New York, NY : Routledge, 2023. |
Series: Giving voice to values, 2578-5060 | Includes bibliographical references and index. |
Identifiers: LCCN 2022059721 (print) | LCCN 2022059722 (ebook) |
ISBN 9781032208879 (hardback) | ISBN 9781032208893 (paperback) |
ISBN 9781003265726 (ebook)
Subjects: LCSH: Corporate culture. | Organizational sociology. |
Corporations—Sociological aspects.
Classification: LCC HD58.7 .C69 2023 (print) | LCC HD58.7 (ebook) |
DDC 302.3/5—dc23/eng/20230104
LC record available at https://lccn.loc.gov/2022059721
LC ebook record available at https://lccn.loc.gov/2022059722

ISBN: 978-1-032-20887-9 (hbk)
ISBN: 978-1-032-20889-3 (pbk)
ISBN: 978-1-003-26572-6 (ebk)

DOI: 10.4324/9781003265726

Typeset in Joanna
by codeMantra

In grateful acknowledgment and appreciation of our families and the organizations that have trusted us in this challenging & meaningful work.

CONTENTS

FOREWORD

Mary C. Gentile, PhD
Creator/Director, Giving Voice to Values, www.MaryGentile.com, www.
GivingVoiceToValues.org
Author of *Giving Voice to Values: How To Speak Your Mind When You Know What's Right*
(Yale University Press, 2010).

In *Authentic Excellence for Organizations: Creating Flourishing "&" Cultures*, R. Kelly
Crace, Charles J. Hardy, and Robert L. Crace have created an inspiring and
practical roadmap and toolkit for building organizational cultures which
are both productive and – dare I say – enjoyable. The entire book is built
upon the identification and healing of counterproductive dichotomies in
our thinking and functioning. Now there are many authors and advisors
who have pointed out the negative impact of dichotomous thinking but
what sets this book apart is its use of real-world scenarios to both illustrate
the frequency and limits of this sort of binary framing of our organizational
experiences but also and even more impactfully, to demonstrate the
application of practical scripts and action plans for countering it.

This wonderfully readable and imminently useful book builds its
approach upon two thinking and behavioral frameworks: *Authentic Excellence*
(AX) and *Giving Voice To Values* (GVV). First of all, the authors reframe each

of the book's organizational challenge scenarios using the *Authentic Excellence* model[1]. Built upon a deep understanding of psychological motivations, AX helps individuals to redefine their objectives and their experience of success and productivity, moving from an exclusive focus on outcomes – which can promote stress and a fear of failure that ironically constrains effectiveness – to a focus upon living in alignment with one's values and deeper purpose and thereby unleashing greater motivation, engagement, and even patience with setbacks.

After redefining the organizational challenge scenarios in this way, the authors apply the *Giving Voice To Values* framework[2] to develop and illustrate examples of actual scripts and an implementation plan for acting upon this new set of objectives. GVV is an innovative approach to values-driven leadership development that moves from the typical emphasis upon building awareness and analysis skills to a focus upon action through pre-scripting, rehearsal, and peer coaching, with a goal of building not only new skills but also new habits, a sort of "moral muscle memory" that makes it more likely that individuals will actually behave in alignment with their values more confidently, more competently, and more comfortably.

When applied to scenarios that address managing stress, balancing an emphasis upon competition with collaboration, valuing innovation as well as tradition, pursuing productivity without sacrificing personal fulfillment, bringing both an emotional and an analytical lens to workplace challenges, and developing both mentorship and followership roles, these two frameworks – AX and GVV – provide readers with tools, scripts, and confidence to enact their values – confidently, more naturally, and effectively. As the creator of GVV, I could not be more pleased and honored to see how the authors have applied the approach, focusing not on preaching but on practice, not on decision-making but on implementation, not on rules and guidelines but on tools.

Notes

1 Crace, R.K. & Crace R.L. (2020). Authentic Excellence: Flourishing and resilience in a Relentless World. New York: Routledge.

2 Gentile, Mary C. (2010) *Giving Voice To Values: How To Speak Your Mind When You Know What's Right*. New Haven, CT: Yale University Press. www.MaryGentile.com, www.GivingVoiceToValues.org

1

INTRODUCTION

AUTHENTIC EXCELLENCE FOR ORGANIZATIONS: CREATING FLOURISHING "&" CULTURES

Marra was starting to wonder what she had gotten herself into. When she was hired as the company's first Chief Wellness Officer, Marra had seen the position as a culmination of all that she had worked toward. Being a successful athlete in college, getting her degree in public health, and an advanced certification in health coaching, she had moved from years of focusing on individual health to exploring how organizational cultures could shift to greater wellbeing. She wanted to go beyond the traditional HR trainings and instill a true paradigm shift in the cultural fabric of an organization. Now she had the ability to do so with her new position – or so she thought. Marra had outlined what she thought was a visionary strategic plan that would help the organization achieve its potential. But in her team meetings with the other leaders and during her first address to the employees, she was met with a bemused reaction. Marra accepted the resistance knowing that change was hard and that it was going to take time for staff to trust and believe the sincerity of her methods.

At a dinner that night with her close friend, Stacey, who had connected her to the job, Marra shared how the employees had reacted. Stacey

DOI: 10.4324/9781003265726-1

had worked for the company for several years before leaving to work at a startup. Stacey smiled as Marra finished explaining her experiences and replied, "Sounds like they were waiting for the 'but.'"

"What do you mean?" Marra asked.

"Take care of yourself, BUT I need this project done by Monday," Stacey responded. She went on to explain the company's reputation for high stress-glorification culture. Stress was seen as a valued barometer of distinction. There was a constant one-upping among staff. Suffering was competitive and the winner would often receive the awards at the end of the year for excellence. It became a running joke among the employees that the award was really the Misery Award.

Once a year, the company would bring someone in to talk about wellness and the CEO would exclaim the importance of self-care. But soon after the wellness workshop — sometimes even on the same day — the CEO would start analyzing the company's progress in relation to their goals and point out someone to laud based on their sacrifice and hard work. Employees interpreted the message of self-care as "throttling back" and in a stress glorification culture, throttling back wasn't an option.

"You know why they created this position, don't you?" Stacey asked. Marra shook her head. "Their biggest competitor hired a Chief Wellness Officer and got all kinds of positive press about it."

"Why didn't you tell me this when you told me about the position?"

Stacey smiled, "Because I figured if anyone could turn this around, it would be you." Marra sipped her bourbon and slid the check across the table. Stacey laughed, adding, "You know you love a challenge."

Organizational Culture from a Values Lens

If you were asked to reflect on the words "organizational culture" what would be the first images that come to mind? Try not to focus on words or a definition, what are the images that come to mind? Who comes to mind? What behaviors reflect organizational culture? What emotions and thoughts come to mind with those images?

Our daily lives are immensely influenced by organizations, partly because of the notion that more can be done and accomplished as a group than as an individual. It's the age-old platitude of "TEAM = Together Everyone Achieves More." Even athletes in individual sports still rely on a team of trainers, coaches, and specialists to optimize their performance. We are a relational species. It's in our DNA to work together.

While it seems intuitive that a group of individuals who work together will be more effective than individuals working on a task by themselves, in most cases, complex issues can only be addressed if a group of individuals work effectively as a team. Finding ways to get teams to work well together is any organizational leader's challenge in achieving sustainable excellence. That's when organizational culture comes into play (Blanchard & Bowles, 1998; Blanchard, Bowles, Darew & Parisi-Carew, 2001; Buckingham, 2005; Katzenbach & Smith, 2003; Kouzes, & Posner, 2007).

The complexity of group effectiveness stems from the complexity of relationships. Starting at the individual level, we are all impacted by the uncertainties and absurdities of our lives. Take a few moments and reflect on all of the influences and experiences that have shaped and informed who you are today. Think of the habits that have developed as a function of living in an uncertain, relentless environment. Some of those habits are healthy, and some are not. Think of the patterns you have developed in how you relate to others, trust others, cope and protect yourself around others, and open up to others. Now bring all those dynamics into an organization where everyone is also bringing their own influences into the mix.

This book explores organizational culture from a values-based perspective. Return to the images that first came to mind when you reflected on organizational culture? What values might those images reveal? And what do we mean when we refer to values? Personal values are beliefs that guide one's behavior, motivation, and decision-making. They also serve as the lens through which we view ourselves and our world. As values develop, they are crystalized and prioritized to form a values system. Individuals act on both personal and common values. Common values refer to those universally held values that serve as the moral and ethical fabric of our behavior, such as respect, honesty, fairness, and compassion. While individuals act on personal and common values, organizations act on common values and collective values – those values that represent what is important to the organization as a whole. Aligning behaviors with values is a challenging task on an individual level, and it is extremely challenging to do on an organizational level. We will examine the tendency for organizations to mismanage the relationship between values and fear, resulting in "Or" cultures that impact productivity, fulfillment, and resilience.

Why Is Organizational Flourishing So Hard?

The Tendency toward "Or" Cultures

There is often a linear assumption between values and effectiveness. That is, if a person or organization stays focused on their values, then it is assumed that motivation and action should fall in line with those values. However, when we dare to care, we become acutely aware of possible "What ifs?" This anticipatory fear is based upon three unavoidable truths around items of importance: uncertainty, perceived costs of failure, and the perceived evaluation of others. These truths can evoke a natural fear of failure which is typically experienced in the form of pressure. Once we feel pressure, there is a tendency to adopt an over-controlling, perfectionistic approach; or an avoidance, procrastination approach.

So, we've learned that there is a dynamic relationship between values and fear. We can't care about anything without being reminded of the uncertainty surrounding what we care about. And we can't fear anything that we don't care about. If we don't manage values-centered fear well, then fear starts to lead, creating a need for reassurance that everything will be okay based on the outcomes of the day. We become very dependent on outcomes or the experiences of the day to reassure that what matters most to us will be okay.

We can't ignore the reality of outcomes in our world. Outcomes are not inherently "bad." They provide us with motivation to maintain our work, rewards for the work we do, and information on our development. However, there is a big difference between desiring outcomes and being desperate for outcomes. Performance psychology suggests that when an outcome is a **want** it tends to work in our favor. When an outcome becomes a **need** it interferes with our performance as it becomes attached to our perception of our self-worth. If we need an outcome, we cannot fail. And if we cannot fail then our fear of failure skyrockets and compels us to behave in ways that negatively impact performance.

Fear of failure leads to fear-based need and power, which negatively impacts values expression and management within organizations. "Or" cultures derive from poor management of natural values tensions. Tensions often arise between opposing dialectics: competitive versus collaborative, innovation versus tradition, independence versus interdependence, analytical versus emotional, etc. Unmanaged fear can exacerbate these natural values tensions. When organizations regularly operate around a fear-based approach, the organization will often prioritize one dynamic to reduce the fear. One side of the tensions will receive more importance than the other side, reducing the values tension to a singular dynamic. These dynamics become rigid and entrenched in the cultural fabric, resulting in ethical vulnerability, marginalization, stagnation, and organizational ineffectiveness.

Research by Google, code named "Project Aristotle" (Duhigg, 2016, 2017), found that what really matters in terms of effectiveness is less about who is on the team and more about how the team works together. This research identified five critical variables for organizational effectiveness, presented in order of importance.

- **Psychological Safety:** An individual's perception of the consequences of taking an interpersonal risk in the face of being seen as ignorant, incompetent, negative, or disruptive. In a team with high psychological safety, teammates feel safe to take risks around their team members. They feel confident that no one on the team will embarrass or punish someone for admitting a mistake, asking a question, or offering a new idea.
- **Dependability:** On dependable teams, members reliably complete quality work on time vs the opposite – shirking responsibilities.
- **Structure and Clarity:** An individual's understanding of job expectations, the process for fulfilling these expectations, and the consequences of one's performance. Goals can be set at the individual or group level, and must be specific, challenging, and attainable.
- **Meaning:** Finding a sense of purpose in either the work itself or the output is important for team effectiveness. The meaning of work is personal and can vary, e.g. financial security, supporting family, helping the team succeed, or individual self-expression.
- **Impact:** The results of one's work, the subjective judgment that your work is making a difference. Seeing that one's work is contributing to the organization's goals can help reveal impact (https://rework. withgoogle.com/guides/understanding-team-effectiveness/steps/ identify-dynamics-of-effective-teams/).

Yet, few organizations develop a culture that is based upon these critical variables. Instead, they often drift into fear reduction dynamics where need and power are prominent, and success is only defined by the outcomes experienced. In the same way we are wired to be relational and work in groups, we are also neurologically compelled to manage fear of failure by tension reduction through over-control (if in a position of power) or avoidance (if in a position of non-power), thereby diminishing organizational effectiveness and healthy teamwork.

Shifting from "Or" to "&" Cultures

Organizations tend to address conflicting needs by prioritizing one dynamic over another. Comfort and efficiency can develop around these prioritized dynamics, but it's an efficiency that tends to favor either/or thinking, or dichotomized thinking. Dichotomized thinking results in the practice of viewing conflicting needs separately and addressing one over the other. Living according to absolutes there is a tendency to become overwhelmed, stressed, and reactive versus proactive, persistence, and patient. Fear-based need and power drive us toward this type of singular thinking. Fortunately, we can choose other methodologies that allow us to manage tensions and embrace complexity.

Dr. Marsha Linehan, who developed Dialectical Behavior Therapy (DBT), uses the term "dialectics" to describe tensions between two seeming opposites (Linehan, 1993). The goal of this approach is to help individuals manage polarities or paradoxes more effectively by moving toward more balanced and integrative responses. When patterns of thinking, feeling, and behaving are reduced to dichotomies, there is usually a degree of imbalance/tension that can be overwhelming and create a need for relief by any means most readily available. In organizations, that can result in reducing the tension by removing one of the opposites and giving validity only to one dynamic in an attempt to "clean" the messiness of ambivalence (Linehan, 1993).

Deborah Scgrieder-Saykbuerm (2014) has a similar view when it comes to paradox thinking. Paradox thinking is "both/&" processing and decision-making. In paradox thinking, pairs of opposites are identified, and a determination is made as to how the polarities are interdependent relative to the aim or goal trying to be achieved. It disrupts the assumption that if a situation is analyzed effectively one option will emerge as the winner. Fear-based need and power often provide the fuel for either/or thinking. The key is to discover patterns of interdependencies. Paradox thinking facilitates balanced management of conflicting objectives and dynamics operative in the organization (Scgrieder-Saykbuerm, 2014).

In Tim Elmore's *Eight Paradoxes of Great Leadership* (2021), he argues that successful leaders are indeed uncommon in that they embrace conflicting demands and seek to balance the following eight paradoxes: Confidence/Humility, Vision/Blind Spots, Visibility/Invisibility, Stubborn/Open-Minded, Personal/Collective, Teachers/Learners, Modeling High Standards/Gracious Forgiveness, and Timely/Timeless. According to Elmore, these uncommon leaders stand out because they are able to balance the tensions created by these paradoxes. Our focus is to expand that embracing of conflicting demands to include all individuals within an organization at a systemic and cultural level.

Transformative Optimizers: Why "&" Cultures Lead to Flourishing

When the focus of an organization shifts from tension reduction to tension management, and when effective strategies are applied to managing fear, need, and power, both sides of singular organizational dynamics are honored. Singular organizational dynamics that are managed well combine to create a new organizational dynamic that elevates the team to an "&" culture and greater effectiveness. It has the effect of transforming a maximizing, fear-based "Or" culture to an optimizing, values-centered "&" culture. These new dynamics that we call "Transformative Optimizers" (TOs) enable a culture of openness and trust where moral, collective, and personal values can be directly attended to and managed. There is a natural tension between the singular dynamics of wellness and stress. As was the case with Marra's company, many organizations will espouse the importance of employee wellness, but crowd out the space for wellness with stress glorification. However, if the dynamics of wellness & stress can be seen as equally valuable and managed well, an elevated dynamic of resilience emerges. Resilience is the TO for wellness & stress. Each chapter of this book will explore the TOs that are a part of each essential "&."

Our Essential "&s"

This book identifies 8 Essential &s and their TOs for organizational flourishing. To qualify as an Essential &, the following criteria were applied:

1. Do organizations commonly experience natural tensions between the two singular dynamics? Do these tensions often emerge as conflicts that require attention?

2. Is there a clear, values-based TO that moves the organization from an Or to an "&" paradigm? Does an elevated, collective dynamic kick in so that effective values management can be developed and practiced, allowing the organization to flourish?

3. Are there practical action steps that can help organizations get to the Essential "&"?

The following are the Essential "&s" that we cover and their TOs

Essential &s	Transformative Optimizers (TOs)
Personal Values & Common Values	Integrity and Inclusion
Competitive & Collaborative	Sustainable Motivation
Stressed & Well	Resilience
Hard & Right	Values-Led Engagement
Innovation & Tradition	Optimal Change Adaptability
Productive & Fulfilled	Meaningful Achievement
Emotional & Analytical	Inclusive 3D Decision-Making
Mentoring & Following	Reciprocal Influence

The Framework

Giving Voice to Values & Authentic Excellence

Giving Voice to Values (GVV). Growing beyond "Or" cultures requires intentional values advocacy for which GVV (Gentile, 2010) provides an effective platform. Mary Gentile's program empowers individuals to imagine, clarify, and actualize stepping into values advocacy. GVV doesn't shy away from the difficulty of leading with one's values but provides a method of developing confidence in doing so. The principles of GVV involve action steps that build healthy and ethical work cultures. Through practice scenarios, members of a group are able to clarify the purpose of acting on their values as well as develop a confidence in aligning their voice with their authentic selves (Gentile, 2010).

Each of our chapters is framed around a GVV process to personalize and internalize the work of creating flourishing "&" cultures. It is adapted from the following GVV process designed to script, practice, and build muscle memory around giving voice to our values with others.

1. **The Ethical Issue** – What is wrong? What are the possibilities for dealing with what is perceived as wrong? "How will I respond to this

issue?" The key to this step is acknowledging that there is a values conflict.

2. **Purpose and Choice** – Reflection about one's personal and professional purpose? "What is my purpose in voicing my values in this situation? What is my Why? What are my choices?"

3. **Process and Data/Stakeholder Analysis** – "What is at stake for others and how do I engage them? Who are my allies and/or key stakeholders?"

4. **Scripting and Acting/Crafting a Powerful Response** – What are potential arguments? "What will I say and do? What are my options? Who are my allies?" Is there any research to do? This step is designed to develop and practice effective GVV scripts and to identify rationalizations, levers, and enablers that facilitate achieving one's purpose. "What does my Game Plan entail and who can I count on for support?"

5. **Scripting and Coaching** –Scripting and practicing enabling conversations with peer coaches. "What will I say or do?" (Chappell, Edwards, & Webb, 2013; Edwards & Kirkham, 2013; Edwards, Webb, Chappell, & Gentile, 2012; Gentile, 2010).

We have adapted this GVV structure to analyze, apply, and practice Organizational Essential &s:

1. **Recognizing the Or Conflict** – What does the Or conflict look like? How do values influence the Or tensions around the two singular dynamics contributing to the conflict?

2. **Finding the Purpose of &** – How can both singular dynamics be honored and applied in the context of an organization? What is the Why behind developing a TO that can lead to a culture of & around these specific dynamics?

3. **Analyzing Your Team** – What do the Or tensions look like specifically in your organization? How are others in the organization experiencing these singular dynamics?

4. **Readying for &: Game Planning** – How can you address Or tensions and apply & strategies so that TOs begin to materialize?

5. **Giving Voice to &: From Game Plan to Action** – What does an organizational game plan look like in action? How can an organization address Or tensions; establish TOs; and create & cultures that lead to organizational flourishing?

Authentic Excellence (AX). From GVVs foundations in creating healthy, ethical work cultures, this book also addresses the psychological complexity of personal and organizational values and its impact on flourishing using the AX framework (Crace & Crace, 2020). The term "Authentic Excellence" reflects a redefinition of productivity based on one's sense of purpose, which is derived from one's values rather than outcomes experienced. Success is seen as the courage to engage in one's values whereby the basis of motivation and decision-making shifts from being fear-centered to values-centered. Shifting from the outcome-oriented, fear-based excellence model to a values-centered focus on engagement can tap into deeper levels of productivity, resilience, and fulfillment – AX.

Flourishing on an individual level can be viewed as the authentic expression and healthy management of one's personal and common values. Flourishing at an organizational level is similar but requires an inclusive, authentic expression and management of collective, common, and differing personal values. When we align our behavior with our values, we increase the probability of living with purpose rather than living at our neurology – patterned responses based on fear and comfort. When groups and individuals develop deeper relationships with their values systems, they improve their ability to build effective coping skills and management strategies. Investigating and building relationships with one's values as a group and in the context of an organization can lead to strategies that promote "&" cultures. When an organization can develop a culture that honors the values and meaning associated with opposing dynamics, a transformative, optimized culture emerges.

By integrating the principles of *GVV* and *AX*, we describe a process that details how organizational members can harness their team's natural wisdom to flourish through the relentless pace and pressure of today's world. How do we create an organizational culture that effectively sustains Me & We? Moving beyond mere team building, the book will help develop a deeper understanding of values-centered cultures and provide strategies and scenarios for creating flourishing teams of equity and effectiveness. The fundamental premise behind the frameworks of both GVV and AX is that it takes practice and work.

Note: The vignettes described throughout the book reflect themes and issues we have experienced with multiple organizations. They do not pertain to any specific organization or person.

References

Blanchard, K., & Bowles, S. (1998). *Gung Ho! Turn on the people in any organization.* William Morrow and Company, Inc.

Blanchard, K., Bowles, S., Darew, D., & Parisi-Carew, E. (2001). *High Five! The magic of working together.* William Morrow.

Buckingham, M. (2005). *The one thing you need to know...About great managing, great leading, and sustained individual success.* Free Press.

Chappell, S., Edwards, M.G., & Webb, D. (2013). Sustaining Voices: Applying giving voices to values to sustainability issues. *Journal of Business Ethics Education, 10,* 211–230.

Crace, R.K., & Crace, R.L. (2020). *Authentic Excellence: Flourishing and resilience in a Relentless World.* Routledge.

Duhigg, C. (February 25, 2016). What Google Learned from Its Quest to Build the Perfect Team. *The New York Times Magazine.*

Duhigg, C. (2017). *Smarter faster better: The transformative power of real productivity.* Random House.

Edwards, M.G., & Kirkham, N. (2013). Situating "Giving Voice to Values": A metatheoretical evaluation of a new approach to business ethics. *Journal of Business Ethics.* https://doi.org/10.1007/s0551-013-1738-7

Edwards, M.G., Webb, D.A., Chappell, S., & Gentile, M.C. (2012). Giving Voice to Values: A new perspective on ethics in globalised organisatonal environments. In C. Wankel & S. Malleck (Eds.), *Ethical models and applications of globalization: Culture, socio-political and economic perspectives* (pp. 160–185). Information Age Publishing.

Elmore, T. (2021). *The eight paradoxes of great leadership. Embracing the conflicting demands of today's workplace.* HarperCollins Leadership.

Gentile, Mary. (2010). *Giving voice to values: How to Speak your mind when you know what's right.* Yale University Press.

Katzenbach, J.R., & Smith, D. (2003). *The wisdom of team. Creating the high-performance organization.* Collins Business.

Kouzes, J.M., & Posner, B.Z. (2007). *The leadership challenge* (4th ed.). John Wiley and Sons, Inc.

Linehan, M.M. (1993). *Cognitive-behavioral treatment of borderline personality disorder.* Guilford Press.

Scgrieder-Saykbuerm, Deborah. (2014). *The power of paradox: Harness the energy of competing ideas to uncover radically innovative solutions.* Career Press.

2

PERSONAL VALUES "&" COMMON VALUES

TRANSFORMATIVE OPTIMIZERS: INTEGRITY AND INCLUSION

Lanley Development was a real estate company started by the great William Lanley in 1973. At the time, the small town of Pikeville consisted of several main street shops and unpaved roads that ventured off into different communities. William Lanley utilized benefits from the GI Bill to build an efficient commercial building several miles from main street. After a couple of years, the building, now buildings, William had developed became the new commercial center of the town. Throughout the 1980's, Lanley Development grew into a strong company with 25 employees. Most of the company's staff were made up of folks from the surrounding area who had similar backgrounds and upbringings to William and his growing family. The staff, along with William, believed in the work they were doing. They were growing the town of Pikeville while providing for their families. Businesses were moving in; residential development tripled; municipalities and schools were added. William's personal values – Achievement, Interdependence, Responsibility, and Financial Prosperity – were shared by much of the staff who were proud to have grown Pikeville into one of the more desirable, up-and-coming towns in the area.

DOI: 10.4324/9781003265726-2

The eldest of William's children, Kyle, began working for the company after graduating college. He admired the sense of fulfillment his Dad and others in the company seemed to derive from their work. Most of the staff Kyle had known his entire life began to reach retirement age or moved on to their own careers. Kyle's Dad, William, allowed Kyle to take on more and more administrative responsibilities because the company was growing at an unprecedented rate. Folks kept moving to Pikeville and Lanley Development kept fostering and benefiting from the growth.

By 2005, when William was ready to retire, the staff at Lanley Development had grown to over 200 members. Kyle stepped into his Dad's role as CEO and President of Operations. After working closely with his father for a dozen years, Kyle knew how to mimic his father's management style. The ideas that differed from his father's approach were mostly design and construction related. So while finally at the helm of the company, Kyle focused on implementing his new design concepts. Management and staff had always seemed to run itself. All he had to do was execute his dad's philosophy: keep the town growing and the company profitable to provide jobs and pay employees on time – simple. However, as the company grew, the old management philosophy seemed to no longer work.

It started with a growing concern among employees regarding gentrification and the environmental impact in neighborhoods where Lanley was recently developing. At first, Kyle was annoyed at having to be pulled away from design and construction work to field the concerns. He didn't understand, "The company is growing. That means more money and stability for everybody in the company." But that iron-clad logic that always work for his father seemed to upset employees even more.

There were other new concerns as well. Staff members were requesting more schedule flexibility. Some wanted to work from home for part of the week claiming issues with childcare. None of his father's staff ever complained about childcare or work hours. Staff members were also expressing frustration in not being able to contribute more creative input in company operations. What was wrong with the creative decisions Kyle was making for the company? Lanley Development was bigger and more profitable than ever. Nobody ever questioned his Dad's creative strategies as long as the company kept growing and making money. What was different? What was he missing? At first he pushed back, doubling down on his father's philosophy, "We're making money and growing. Your jobs are secure and well-paid for. That should be enough."

But clamping down on his father's values so he could get back to his design focus backfired. Some folks quit. Staff turnover and new hires wound up occupying much of Kyle's time. The company started receiving unfavorable write ups in local op-eds. Lanley began to garner the reputation of an insensitive company displacing folks from neighborhoods where they had lived for decades. His father never had to deal with these issues. Yet Kyle was blamed for all the problems when he operated the company the same way his father had.

Kyle tried raising salaries. He accommodated some of the staff's unconventional schedule requests. He even set up and funded a nonprofit in hopes of addressing gentrification concerns in the community. But still: there was frequent staff turnover; folks struggled with childcare; staff wanted more creative input; folks even claimed that the non-profit was performative and did little to protect the people who were getting priced out of their neighborhoods.

Nothing Kyle did seemed to work. If you looked on paper, the company was more profitable than it had ever been. Two hundred employees were well paid and working for one of the largest companies in the state. However, judging by the tone in the office, the reputation in the community, and the constant staff turnover; you'd think Lanley Development was crumbling. Kyle didn't know what to do to turn things around.

Step 1. Recognizing the Or Conflict: Is There Really No "I" in "Team?"

Most organizations laud the importance of values and often include a mission, vision, and values statement as a basis for their guiding principles. Values have been shown to be important points of motivation, focus, decision-making, integrity, and ethics (Blanchard & Bowles, 1998; Brown & Crace, 1996; Crace & Hardy, 1997; Kotter, 2012). So, being values-centered makes sense for organizations. Yet, if not properly managed, there are several dynamics associated with being values-centered that can result in confusion and tension. Values can be common and/or personal. Indeed, when people are asked to list their core moral and ethical values there is a great deal of commonality among the listed values. On the other hand, when individuals are invited to identify values that do not carry an inherently moral aspect, there is a lot of disparity among the values listed. For example, the work of Rushworth Kidder (2005) suggests that there is a small set of shared or common values across different contexts that includes honesty, respect, responsibility, fairness, and compassion. While we might argue about which values make "the list" of universal common values, the work of Donaldson and Dunfee (1999) points to the conclusion that common values are the universal "hypernorms" that guide moral and ethical decision-making and behavior. Knowing that certain values can be widely shared provides a foundation to address moral and ethical conflicts.

For example, the collective values of an organization can commonly be more of a reflection of the personal values of the leader(s) using positional power as the basis for the collective values culture. What happens if individuals within that organization do not share the same personal values as the leader? Does that mean that recruitment of staff should be limited to those who share the same personal values as the leader? Defining an organization's values solely by the lens of its leader's values can negatively impact a sense of inclusion for those whose values don't perfectly align with its leader. It can become a culture that is framed by power rather than a true values culture that is based on an aggregate of everyone's values.

Mary Gentile's work on *Giving Voice to Values* (Gentile, 2010) provides a useful framework for empowering individuals and organizations to voice and act on common or shared values in the workplace. While common values can be more consistent across time and culture, personal values have a social context and therefore have a level of social "should" associated with them. During our work on the development of the *Life Values Inventory* (Brown & Crace, 1996; Crace & Brown, 1996; Brown & Crace, 2002; Crace & Brown, 2002; Crace, 2012) we found moral and ethical values – virtues that had an obvious social should or moral weight – did very little to distinguish among individuals because so many people endorse these types of values as high, regardless of whether they were acting on them or not. Values assessments are vulnerable to being only a picture of values that have the most positive weight rather than a true picture of what matters to the person at the time of the assessment. We were interested in connecting an individual's values to their behavior when determining what matters to them, not just reminding them of the social "should."

Aligning behaviors with values is perhaps one of the most challenging tasks that organizations face. One way organizations seek this alignment is to focus both on common moral values and collective values that reflect an aggregate of personal values. If we can agree on a set of common and collective values, we then can create shared goals.

But how do you create a culture that honors and respects the values of each member and still provides a direction and focus for decision-making and motivation? Prioritization of values is as critical as crystallization of values (Crace & Crace, 2020) in order for an organization to use values effectively. Values crystallization is assessing the prominent values in an organization; values prioritization is ranking them in terms of most and least important. Prioritization of collective values illuminates values that have the strongest cultural traction and that tap into intrinsic motivation. So, it's not enough to clarify collective values but it's important to create a collective order of those values that are the most guiding principles of an organization's work environment.

What if an organization focuses only on personal and collective values at the exclusion of moral or common values? An organization can be values-centered without a moral compass. An organization can have Achievement as its highest collective value but without a moral compass they could embrace "the ends justify the means" approach to acting on that value. The exploration of an organization's values culture that is inclusive of everyone's personal values is, frankly, extremely difficult, time consuming, and uncomfortable. It is much easier to clean up the complexity by letting the leader's personal values dictate the values culture; focusing only on personal values without diving into the emphasis of a moral and ethical compass; or ignoring the discussion of values altogether. When values are placed in an "Or" paradigm for reasons of comfort or simplicity, they cease to provide a powerful force of motivation, focus, and ethical decision-making. When these positive factors of values are reduced, values start to become tools of judgment or silencing.

Looking at the Lanley Development example, when William ran the company much of the staff naturally aligned with William's direction. William's personal values of Achievement, Interdependence, Responsibility, and Financial Prosperity were also the collective values of that particular staff. At the time William was growing the company, the staff was smaller and of a similar background and worldview as William. The direction of the company aligned with the personal, collective, and moral values of those who comprised the company. As time progressed and Kyle took over the company, a larger group of staff members made up a larger collection of differing personal values and moral concerns that did not align with the older collective values of the company. These older collective values that originated from William and the initial staff were being imposed by Kyle not necessarily because they reflected his own personal values, but because it was a precedent that had grown the company to financial prosperity. This was a goal that was no longer the only priority of the company's staff.

Step 2. Finding the Purpose of &: Building a Culture of Integrity and Inclusion

What is the benefit of creating a cultural space that honors personal, collective, and moral values? An organization's culture will reflect what it spends the most time discussing and acting upon. Taking the time to explore a more complex look at values sends the message that values will be the predominant driver of a team's behavior, motivation, and decision-making. If values are rarely reviewed or limited to the values of the positional leader, then the priority will be focused on something other than values – most typically fear-based urgencies or practices that are comfortable and familiar. Taking the time to understand and respect the values of all individuals within the organization and creating an aggregate of all staff's values leads to a greater sense of inclusion, even for those whose values are not completely satisfied within that organization.

Furthermore, by leading and developing organizational goals from values, behavior is likely to become more aligned with values which increases a sense of integrity. One of the cornerstones of adult self-esteem and resilience is integrity – the alignment of our behavior with our values. An organization can function with integrity – rather than intention – when it takes the time to deeply understand the values that are driving the team, develops goals from those values, and provides pathways for attaining those goals. It's imperative for an organization to operationally define integrity in a way that is based on the driving values of the organization; as a result, integrity looks different for every organization.

This kind of individual and collective values assessment within the context of team creates a level of openness to values discussions, which can pave a way to the discussion of moral or common values. The discussion of moral values can be uncomfortable and result in avoidance or shame-based judgment from those in positional power. A repeated values discussion honors a priority on personal values and creates space for the honest acknowledgment of common and moral values. While there are cultural influences and personal experiences that shape the prioritization of values, there are some values that are deemed moral foundations that extend beyond an individual context.

Crafting a Personal & Common Purpose

By devoting time and energy to understanding the operational function of common values as well as those of the team and individuals, organizations can experience and utilize fulfillment. Fulfillment comes from engaging in authentically held values. By assessing and crystallizing a team's values, organizations can find a means for measuring fulfillment. Shared and individual goals can develop from values, and productivity can stem from those goals. Values-centered goal setting evokes a deeper sense of fulfillment by tapping into purpose. Purpose can be common as well as personal – individual and organizational. Including both personal and common values will allow both the individual and the organization to flourish because the moral compass points individuals and the organization in the right direction.

Embracing Moral Leadership

Moral leadership refers to conduct that exemplifies strong common values. Decision-making in moral leadership is guided by a moral purpose/ compass. Common values are a core component of a healthy organizational culture. An organization that has a set code of ethics in place benefits from motivated employees and better individual performance. Organizations with effective moral leadership consist of members who don't abuse power. In addition, leaders who have morals and ethics have integrity, are inclusive, and put organizational needs before their own. Let's refer back to the Lanley Development example, Kyle didn't exhibit glaring signs of toxic leadership, but there were growing misalignments that were causing tension among personal, collective, and moral values that the staff members now prioritized: Concern for Others – longtime residents being priced out of their neighborhoods – and Concern for Environment were values that Kyle was not honoring at the level staff members felt the company was morally obligated to do. When Kyle's father, William, was running the company, most of the moral, collective, and personal values of the company—Financial

Prosperity and Responsibility—naturally aligned. At the time, the smaller, less diverse group of staff members viewed the direction of the company, their personal lives, and moral objectives similarly.

Moral leadership is fundamental to organizational flourishing. It helps maintain and encourage teamwork, performance, and morale by establishing a healthy culture of integrity and inclusion. Moral leadership displays the following characteristics:

Emotional intelligence. One of the most significant characteristics of moral leadership is emotional intelligence. Emotional intelligence is defined as an individual's ability to read, understand, and manage their own emotions while also recognizing and influencing the emotions of those in their presence. Emotional intelligence is one of the most important skills a leader can have in any organization. People with high emotional intelligence exhibit proactive behavior and are adept at resolving conflicts within any organization. Leaders with emotional intelligence tend to create a culture of collaboration across the organization. Indeed, research indicates that emotional intelligence promotes trust and trust fosters a collaborative culture which enhances the creativity and performance of the team (Barczak, Lassk, and Mulki, 2010; Druskat & Wolff, 2001; Goleman, 2005; Landry, 2019).

Integrity and inclusion. Leaders consistently doing what they say they will do best display moral leadership. Simply put, their actions match their words and they live their values. Moral leaders demonstrate integrity and inclusion. They make others feel valued, embrace differences, honor commitments, and follow through on their promises. Moral leaders hold themselves to a high ethical standard striving to embrace common values over personal gain or individual profit. They hold themselves and others to a set of common moral and ethical values.

Balancing common and personal values. Moral leadership means understanding how your own principles and values align with common values and those of the organizations they belong to. When business leaders embody the values of an organization and take responsibility for the consequences of their actions, they inspire team members to do the same.

Calibrating the moral compass for personal & common values. In this approach, the focus is on helping the organization maintain its moral compass. A moral compass points the organization in its right direction. Not only does a moral compass assist in defining ethical boundaries, it helps us act in a moral and ethical manner regardless of the context (Bennett, 1995; Thompson, 2009). A moral compass is a tool that appeals to a universal higher sense of right/good within members of an organization – common values. As a tool, the moral compass also enables the organization to do the right thing for the right reasons while leading individuals to be authentic in acting on their values – personal values. Rather than focus on one or the other (common or personal), we suggest focusing on common, individual, and collective values. The key to creating a moral compass is to create an organization that is committed to acting on personal and organizational values as well as common values. The moral compass serves as a guardrail to guide motivation and behavior.

Step 3. Analyzing Your Team – Assessing the Me, the We, and the Morality

After several years of high staff turnover and a waning reputation throughout the community, Kyle hired a consultant to help broaden his organization to include the collective values of the staff and reconfigure the company's objectives.

Collective Values Assessment

- Go to the open educational resource (OER) website, www.lifevaluesinventory.org. (or utilize the LVI assessment in the Appendix).
- Go to the Group Leaders portal and create a personalized URL link for the organization. For larger organizations, sub-links can be created that are specific to departments or working groups.
- Using the personalized URLs, team members will go through an individual assessment of their values and receive an individualized report of their current relationship with their values.
- By using the personalized URLs, everyone's individual results will be integrated into a collective aggregate, depicting the most prominent collective values.

Upon creating a collective values assessment, the top four values from the collective aggregate were Creativity, Concern for Others, Financial Prosperity, and Concern for the Environment. Kyle hadn't realized an inclusive opportunity that had been there all along – Creativity. He had been continuing with his father's personal values as a management precedent because it had worked, but even he didn't align with all his father's personal values. Kyle had always valued Creativity more than his father. Opportunities for creative designs, construction, and business strategies had always interested him. Now he saw that he was a part of an entire company who also valued Creativity. How could this natural alignment bridge the gap to other clearly important values like Concern for Others and Concern for the Environment? How could the company direct its endeavors to fulfill Concern for Others and Concern for the Environment and in so doing build integrity?

Step 4. Readying for &: Game Plan for Integrity & Inclusion

Inclusion Exercise: Getting to Know each Other through the Lens of Personal Values

In a group setting, divide team members into pairs and have them share the answers to the following questions about their values profile. Change partners after each question. These questions take a while to work through and are conducive to retreat settings. For meetings of smaller duration, the team can pick a few questions of most interest.

Reflections on High Priority Values

What's great and positive about having these values high in your ranking?

What's stressful about having these values high in your ranking?

What were the influences that shaped these values (e.g., cultural, experiential, generational influences)?

How do these values get expressed? How would others know that they are important to you? What does a healthy expression of these values look like for you?

How new or old do these values feel for you? Would they have been among your top values a few years ago? Do you think they will be your top values a few years from now?

How do your high priority (HP) values compare to others in your family, your friends, and your current community?

What fears are attached to your most important values and how do you manage/cope with those fears?

What values feel most comfortable to express in your current environment?

What values feel most difficult to express in your current environment?

Reflections on all 14 Values

What value is currently causing you the most fulfillment and why?

What value is currently causing you the most stress and why?

What value has changed the most for you in the last year?

What value do you hope to affect the most in the next year and how?

What value do you gravitate to during times of change or extreme stress? How does that work well for you, how does it present challenges?

What personal value(s) reflect your family culture and what value(s) represent a departure?

What value(s) are you hardest on yourself and others in terms of judgment?

If you could only be remembered for 3 values, what would they be and how are they currently expressed?

Look at your Over-Attended values. Why are you acting on these values more than you would prefer? What are the underlying purposes calling you to act on these values?

If you could only choose one, what value in your Under-Attended category would you be willing to devote a little more time and energy to?

Are there values in your medium/low priority category that you feel others negatively judged because of their lower importance? Where is that judgment coming from and why?

Are the relationships where a low priority value for you is an HP value for others? How do you navigate that difference in values priority in the relationship?

Stories help us internalize and understand experiences with greater depth. The questions in this exercise are intended to help you create a story about the relationship with your values. Deep, healthy relationships have stories attached to them. Ask a person to describe a relationship and then ask that person to tell a story about the relationship, there will often be a difference in the way that person engages or expresses a sense of meaning. We want the same level of engagement and meaning with values.

As we go through life, it is important to reassess each year how our experiences integrate to inform who we are and where we want to go. These stories shape our relationship with our values and influence our decision-making. But, in the same manner that a good story begs to be shared with others, it's important to share the reflections of your values with teammates and inquire about their values-relationship stories. When you organize your thoughts into a conversational story that others understand, you move into another level of understanding. And when you ask the same questions of others, hear their stories, and reflect on the impact of those stories, you move into an even deeper level of understanding with your own values. This deepening of comprehension through story increases the probability that your values will become a primary source of motivation, a motivation that surpasses mood, fatigue, and fear. Understanding the story of your values-relationship calls your values to lead and your fears to follow – in a world where the reverse is common. Furthermore, working in an organization where your values are understood, respected, and affirmed only deepens the level of inclusion and investment into that organization.

Integrity Exercise – Aligning Behavior with Collective Values

As a group, review the Collective Values Assessment that reflects the aggregate of everyone's individual values results. Break up into smaller groups of 5–8 or by departments or work teams.

High Priority Values

High Priority (HP) values are the values that are currently important to the team and are acted on frequently. These are values of integrity because you are walking the walk by acting on what matters most. HP values are a source of fulfillment and meaning. However, values are a double-edged sword because while they are our highest source of fulfillment, they are also a high source of stress.

Additionally, we are vulnerable to needing equity from our HP values. These values are important to us and we are putting in the effort to frequently act on them. It's natural to want a return on that investment of time, energy, and care. The key is to want a fair return without needing it or feeling entitled to it. Otherwise, fear starts to slide to the foreground and values start to move into a need state.

Discuss in small groups how the team's HP values are meaningful and stressful. How they are expressed in a healthy manner and an unhealthy manner? Clarify what each HP value looks like in action, and when that value is expressed in healthy and unhealthy ways.

Over-Attention Values

Over-Attention (OA) values are values that are currently being given more attention than is preferred. We often experience more stress from these values than joy. For very real and understandable reasons, fear is leading with these values and there can be a level of insecurity or worry attached to them. We are vulnerable to feeling insecure about a value when we are outcome-oriented and don't feel confident that we will secure that outcome. We can excessively worry about the outcome, which is a form of over-attention. Whenever we're devoting more attention to a value than we would prefer, the outcome can start to feel like a "have to" or a need, which elevates stress.

Discuss in small groups the reasons why the organization is devoting extra attention to these values and the cost of such over-attention. What would a healthy expression of these values look like?

Under-Attention Values

Your Under-Attention (UA) values are values that are getting less attention than preferred. We tend to experience guilt or sadness around these values. There are typically two reasons why we put values in this category. First, it can be because we are truthfully devoting less time to a value than we believe we should. Second, we are applying a perfectionistic standard to a value. We are seeing that value in terms of its potential in our lives, e.g., "I work out three times a week, but I could always be working out more."

Discuss in small groups the impact of having these values in the under-attention category. If only one value from this category could elevate in importance and attention, which value would that be and why?

Medium/Low Priority Values

Like HP values, medium/low priority values are currently in a place of integrity. Behavior is aligned with their relative importance. Relative to other values, these values have moderate to low importance and there is acceptance with acting on them periodically.

Discuss in small groups the impact of having these values as medium/low priority within the organization.

In small groups, discuss how individuals whose HP values are a part of the organization's medium/low priority values can find healthy ways to express their values within and outside of the organization.

As the groups bring their discussions into the larger group, make note of common themes that emerge for each values category. Feel free to personalize the names and definitions of values that align with the normative culture. For instance, a group may decide that a better term for Responsibility for them is Dependability. It's okay to personalize the values to the organization.

Emerging Moral Priorities

In the final discussion of collective values, identify the collective values that strike a moral tone the group feels extends beyond the organization and connects to a societal good. Highlight these values to distinguish an added layer of importance to these values. For each collective value, distill the input from the groups into a few essential action steps that align collective and common values to organizational behavior.

With the values that have a moral thread, spend time discussing what these values may look like within the current organizational culture. Have each group develop a scenario that would reflect a drift or a violation of those values. Break into peer dyads, choose a scenario, and practice how they may bring attention to a value that is being violated. Process the experience in small groups and then as a large group. Allow this experience to further refine the behaviors and action steps that will serve as the organization's guiding principles.

Step 5. Giving Voice to &: From Game Plan to Action

Following the collective values assessment of the Lanley team, the consultant held a workshop to discuss what the group's collective values looked like in action. Creativity proved to be a fertile common ground where practices could be derived to accommodate values like Concern for Others and Concern for the Environment. However, Kyle and other Lanley executives were surprised to see the aggregate of collective values list Financial Prosperity and Responsibility as top five priority values. These had always been top values in the operation of the company. Kyle's Dad, William, and staff members from the 70s, 80s, and 90s all shared a common goal to grow the company's profitability and through that work provide for their families. Kyle expressed his confusion during a group exercise, "Responsibility and Financial Prosperity have always been the top priorities of this company. Employees have been responsibly providing for their families for generations through their work at Lanley — which is funded by the profits we make. You've all been fighting me tooth and nail when I make max-profit decisions for the company."

"Responsibility doesn't just mean to one's family and company." A recently promoted executive responded.

Many staff members began to nod and agree. Someone stood up and posed, "Don't we have a moral obligation to this town?"

Kyle responded, "This town consisted of two blocks of Main Street and dirt roads before this company."

"But it's been much bigger for the past 30 years. We are responsible for the communities living in Pikeville." Another staff member argued.

"Lanley put Pikeville on the map." An older employee countered, "My work here allowed me to raise a family and put two kids through college. Keeping Lanley profitable, keeps us — and our families going."

"Not everybody's family." A group member blurted out.

Another added, "The whole town doesn't work for Lanley. What about them?"

The executive who'd begun the discussion concluded to Kyle and the group, "We want the company to be strong but not at the detriment of others. That is responsible behavior. Affording one's life and supporting one's family at the expense of another's ability to do the same isn't Financial Prosperity."

The consultant jumped in and suggested an exercise, "Ok, right now I want everybody to write down their own definitions of Responsibility and Financial Prosperity in context to their work at Lanley."

The consultant prompted them to write out a few more answers, "What are the main arguments against your definitions of Responsibility and Financial Responsibility? And, what are the reasons and rationalizations you need to address?"

The staff members were then asked, "When it comes to Responsibility and Financial Prosperity, what's at stake for the key parties including those who disagree with you? What's at stake for you?"

The staff and executives then broke into groups and discussed their definitions, concerns, and ideas. The collective redefinitions allowed the executive management team to develop plans of action over the next year. If the company could align their practices and objectives with the personal, collective, and moral values of its vast staff, it could steer the company in a direction that truly served its staff, financial health, and community.

The group spent time identifying scenarios that would suggest a drift from the moral commitment to how the organization was defining Responsibility. They broke into pairs and practiced how they would raise awareness to violations in Responsibility and then processed this experience in small groups. Then they came together as a full team and further affirmed the personal, collective, and moral importance of Lanley growing into the value of Responsibility inclusively and with integrity. Kyle pointed out how their collective value of Creativity served as a conduit for growth when defining and creating action plans around values.

Kyle developed a task force of creatives to focus on environmental initiatives in the community. The company funded fellowships and hired environmental experts to develop and train members of staff and community on creative permaculture solutions and the interdependencies of environmental, social, and economical influences. Another creative task force was developed to enact projects directly informed by community outreach. Kyle and his design team relished the creative task of developing construction projects needed in under-served communities like state-of-the-art recreation and wellness centers, affordable housing, and municipal works that improved the quality of life in the neighborhoods Lanley had previously been developing for max-profit, commercial, and residential use.

The environmental and community initiatives Lanley Development enacted began to draw attention. After two years, Lanley's innovative, wellness practices in development had garnered national, and in some cases, international acclaim. Folks from around the country wanted to come work for Lanley. Other development corporations applied similar initiatives and their own communities. Lanley's staff grew to over 300 employees as they expanded these practices into neighboring areas. The executive staff Kyle had assembled was made up a diverse group of people with different backgrounds, values, and moral definitions of those values. With regular workshops designed to aggregate and define collective values, the executive team was able to steer company practices in a direction that included the values of its staff and empowered the integrity of their work.

References

Barczak, G., Lassk, F., & Mulki, J. (2010, November 14). Antecedents of team creativity: An examination of team emotional intelligence, team trust and collaborative culture. *Creativity and Innovation Management, 19*(4), 332–345. https://doi.org/10.1111/j.1467-8691.2010.00574.x

Bennett, W.J. (Ed.). (1995). *Moral compass: stories for a life's journey.* Simon and Schuster.

Blanchard, K., & Bowles, S. (1998). *Gung Ho! Turn on the people in any organization.* William Morrow and Company, Inc.

Brown, D., & Crace, R.K. (1996). Values in life role choices and outcomes: A conceptual model. *The Career Development Quarterly, 44*(3), 211–223. https://doi.org/10.1002/j.2161-0045.1996.tb00252.x

Brown, D. & Crace, R.K. (2002). *Life Values Inventory: Facilitator's Guide.* Applied Psychology Resources, Inc. www.lifevaluesinventory.com

Crace, R.K. (2012). *Life Values Inventory Online* (www.lifevaluesinventory.org). Life Values Inventory Online, Inc.

Crace, R.K., & Brown, D. (1996). *Life Values Inventory.* Life Values Resources.

Crace, R.K., & Brown, D. (2002). *Life Values Inventory* (Revised ed.). Applied Psychology Resources.

Crace, R.K., & Brown, D. (1993). *Life values inventory: Clarifying your personal truth.* Applied Psychology Resources, Inc. www.lifevaluesinventory.og.

Crace, R.K., & Crace, R.L. (2020). *Authentic excellence: Flourishing and resilience in a relentless world.* Routledge.

Crace, R.K., & Hardy, C.J. (1997). Individual values and the team building process. *Journal of Applied Sport Psychology, 9*(1), 41–60. https://doi.org/10.1080/10413209708415383

Donaldson, T., & Dunfee, T.W. (1999). *Ties that bind: A social contracts approach to business ethics.* Harvard Business School Press.

Druskat, V.U., & Wolff, S.B. (2001, March). Building the emotional intelligence of groups. *Harvard Business Review,* https://hbr.org/2001/03/building-the-emotional-intelligence-of-groups

Gentile, M.C. (2010). *Giving voice to values: How to speak your mind when you know what's right.* Yale University Press.

Goleman, D. (2005). *Emotional intelligence: Why it can matter more than IQ.* Bantam Books.

Kidder, R.M. (2005). *Moral courage: Taking action when your values are put to the test.* William Morrow.

Kotter, J.P. (2012). *Leading change.* Harvard Business Review Press.

Landry, L. (2019, April 3). *Why emotional intelligence is important in leadership.* Harvard Business School Online, https://online.hbs.edu/blog/post/emotional-intelligence-in-leadership

Thompson, L.J. (2009). *The moral compass: Leadership for a free world.* Information Age Publishing.

3

COMPETITIVE "&" COLLABORATIVE

TRANSFORMATIVE OPTIMIZER: SUSTAINABLE MOTIVATION

The Stallions had no chance of making the playoffs. The pro soccer team was a mix of underperforming youngsters and veterans at the tail end of their careers. The team's facilities were outdated and often in need of repair. On top of all their problems, their star player was now out with a season-ending injury.

The losing was getting out of hand when they hired a new coach, Kat Jenkins, whose reputation was unconventional at best. Fans of the Stallions as well as members of the team saw the hire as yet another clueless move by an apathetic owner.

Kat did little on her first day. She entered the locker room. The players and team personnel stopped and waited for an introductory speech, but all Kat said was, "Hi," before walking into a dank office and turning on a TV.

It went on like that for several days. Kat wandering around the team casually observing while the assistant coaches handled most of the game planning.

In the locker room during halftime of yet another losing match, Robyn, one of the rookie players, stormed right up to one of the veteran players,

DOI: 10.4324/9781003265726-3

"What are you doing!?" The veteran player rolled her shoulders back ready for the confrontation. "I've been open four freaking times and you don't pass? I know you see me."

"What happened last time?" The veteran referenced an open shot Robyn had missed during the previous game.

A more indifferent teammate chimed in, "Why not pass her the ball? We're down by three."

"I'm protecting her from herself. You don't want to get labeled as someone who chokes when there's a wide-open shot." The veteran argued.

Robyn sauntered up to the veteran, "You keep hogging the ball and making the entire offense run through you because you can't accept that you're past it." Face to face the players glared at each other. Robyn added, "I don't think you can cross the ball like you used to. I don't think you have any business being on the field. I don't think you were ever near as good as you think you were–" The veteran shoved Robyn and the rest of the team joined the tussle using the locker room mayhem as an excuse to fight team members they'd been frustrated with all season. Assistant coaches tried pulling players off of each other, but the fighting continued.

Kat exited her office and nonchalantly stepped around the melee until she got to the dry erase board. She hadn't done any coaching since she arrived two weeks ago. So as she started to draw something on the dry erase board the tussling began to settle. Players were curious as to what this strange, uninvolved coach's first deliberate communication would be.

While drawing what looked to be a field diagram, but it wasn't of a soccer field, Kat asked the group that had now settled into silence, "Any of y'all know how to play cricket?" She continued to draw and outline of a cricket pitch. "So this is the bowling crease. The bowler is like a pitcher and they throw it at the wickets which are protected by a batsman..." Kat continued to draw and explain the game of cricket. The players looked around questioning the mental stability of their coach.

Step 1. Recognizing the OR Conflict: Competition – Fuel, Water, or Laxative?

Outcomes are an integral part of how organizations measure progress and success. Without successful outcomes, an organization is not sustainable. But what do organizations rely on to motivate staff toward successful outcomes? Do they pit staff against staff creating an internally competitive environment? Do they create competition with other organizations in the industry to motivate staff? Or do they focus more on a collaborative attainment of outcomes? Do they create a teambuilding culture that prioritizes process-oriented goals? And are outcomes the primary focus or the result of process-oriented goals?

There is a tendency for organizations to either create a competitive culture around outcomes or to create a more collaborative approach. The reason for this tendency is that outcomes are beyond our complete control. There is always uncertainty, and with uncertainty comes fear. Because we have a natural tendency to manage fear through over-control or avoidance, many organizations will either focus on the intensity of competition or they will focus on collaboration – mistakenly believing it to be an easier concentration.

Whether the focus is on competition, collaboration, or both, we know that the approach we take to managing outcomes will impact motivation. While fear and comfort are our most natural motivators on a daily basis, what impacts motivation over time? Is it creating a series of ongoing crises and conflicts to kick in fear as motivation? Or is it creating an environment of positive emotions so that people will be motivated from a place of comfort?

Competition at its essence is a strategic, intentional conflict. That's not a bad thing in and of itself. In fact, for some, it is a powerful motivator – competition providing fuel to their drive. They seek the discomfort and the intensity of competition. There are others who are accepting of competition as being a natural part of their environment but it's not the primary impetus of their work. It's not a fuel for their motivation but is a part of the hydration that keeps them engaged in their environment. For others, competition can create such anxiety that even the anticipation of an upcoming competitive situation wreaks havoc on the gut. The Stallions had defined their worth by wins/losses and by that standard, during their discouraging season the win/loss record no longer served as a form of motivation. Instead, it served to fuel further conflict and frustration, rather than motivation. By the time an athlete reaches a professional level, we know they have tremendous experience managing competition and outcomes. But even professional athletes are vulnerable to the paralyzing effects of perfectionistic expectations derived from others or themselves. And we find tremendous variability even among professional athletes as to how much power they give to outcomes as it relates to their motivation. For some, it's everything; for others, it's *a* factor, but not *the* factor.

Focusing only on collaboration when the motivation is to avoid conflict tends to not be an effective source of motivation over time. First of all, authentic collaboration is really difficult and can be just as tense and frictional as competition. It requires time, patience, courage, and an ability to work with a wide range of perspectives (Brown, 2018). For many organizations, collaboration ends up looking more like cooperation. And while there are benefits to cooperation, the act is more about "helping" without owning a shared responsibility. Cooperation can be safe and comfortable, but it's not collaboration. In order to establish a culture of collaboration, a group has to truly engage in mutual ownership of responsibility where success and disappointment are shared experiences. For the Stallions, the over-emphasis on their record had created a team dynamic that was not competitive, collaborative, nor cooperative.

Step 2. Finding the Purpose of &: Diverse Motivations

Honoring both competition and collaboration elevates an organization by acknowledging that team members can be motivated by different factors. Motivation is a function of four primary factors: thoughts, feelings, energies, and abilities. Our thought patterns and emotions impact whether we are more or less motivated. Our life experiences and values shape our thoughts and feelings, and subsequently, our motivation. Our level of energy or fatigue can also impact our motivation. And the interaction of our current abilities and our current demands can impact motivation both positively and negatively. The Stallions believed the only worthy goal was winning. But because that demand was exceeding their current collective abilities, a blend of conflicting thoughts and feelings deeply impacted their motivation and energy.

Taking the time to understand what shapes and fuels a person's motivation and then incorporating that into the goal-setting of an organization can result in more sustainable motivation. But it's hard work and takes time to build a coherent system that honors each individual's motivation. The overall goal is to tap into the values that have more importance to each individual because values are our deepest form of motivation. But values can be confused with preferences and needs. Preferences are wants that lack the psychological commitment necessary to serve as sustainable motivation. Needs reflect values that have become eclipsed by fear, creating over-attention to certain goals at the expense of other important values. To be sustainable, values require commitment to keep fear from over-influencing that value. It's important to deconstruct each individual's goals in order to distinguish preferences, values, and needs. Then bring together the aggregate values and goals to create a team profile for motivation.

Two values that significantly impact motivation and decision-making are Independence and Interdependence. Independence as a value is defined by the importance of having a sense of autonomy over one's decisions and actions. People who highly value Independence are motivated by opportunities that reward autonomous decision-making and self-reliance. They often view other people as comparative standards to judge how well they are doing. Interdependence is defined by valuing the expectations of one's social group, family, or team. People who highly value Interdependence are motivated to understand and attend to the expectations of others around them. They often prefer collaboration and can judge themselves by how well they are contributing to a team effort. Both values and perspectives have their worth within organizations. And individuals come by these values honestly. So there needs to be space within an organization to honor both. Establishing a harmonious platform of collaboration that also recognizes the distinct uniqueness of each individual's contribution is critical for sustainable motivation. How might tension between independence and interdependence impact collaboration and subsequently motivation? Let's consider another example outside of sports:

The nurses were worn out. In a break room at 3AM, nurses vented to each other, "This place is a bureaucratic mess."

"I'm on a 14-day stint and Sandra still asked me to come in tomorrow."

Sandra, the office manager for the hospital's Endocrinology Division, struggled to hit staggering efficiency goals. She imposed time limitations on patient visits, restructured team personnel, and accommodated most scheduling demands; but all her tactics seemed to create more tension between nurses, aids, physicians, surgeons, administration, specialty skills...

In the break room an RN brought up the team's lead physician, "Did you hear Dr. Waltrip's diagnosis of Mr. Eckard?"

"Let me guess."

"Thyroid Disease," a couple of nurses said in unison.

Another nurse added Dr. Waltrip's standard treatment program for his usual diagnosis, "Six weeks on Beta blockers then a follow up?"

The group nodded.

"It's Type 1 diabetes." The RN theorized.

"Much easier to diagnose thyroid disease and prescribe Beta Blockers." A nurse responded.

Other nurses added their frustrations, "I can't stand watching these rich physicians get rewarded for phoning in diagnoses."

"Makes the hospital more money."

"We get treated like we're the problem for trying to get patients what they actually need."

"You're slowing things down with all your patient advocacy," a nurse cynically joked.

The next morning, Dr. Waltrip gathered a few nurses in the hallway. "Why wasn't the patient in Room 103 discharged?"

A Nurse Practitioner responded, "We needed to run more tests."

Dr. Waltrip rubbed his brow, "You all need to stop second-guessing every one of my diagnoses." He tried to contain his irritation, "We're getting backlogged with patients that don't need to be here."

Sandra was walking by when she heard one of the RN's timidly challenge Dr. Waltrip, "There were signs of diabetic ketoacidosis." Dr. Waltrip started to agitate. The RN rushed to add, "We just want to get it right. These patients are already—"

"Yes, but you think all my diagnoses are wrong." Dr. Waltrip interrupted, "I'm not as negligent as you all make me out to be."

Before Dr. Waltrip's frustration began to boil, Sandra stepped in, "You all need to learn to work as a team," Looking at the nurses, she asserted, "You have to trust each other, or this department's budget will keep getting cut." She briefly glanced at Dr. Waltrip before looking back at the nurses, "If we're not shortening post-op patient days; if we're not following efficient treatment plans; if we are not working together, we don't make money." She paused considering whether to hold back information that kept her up at night, "If we don't make money, we help less people. No margin, no mission."

Sandra thought she saw one of the RT's role his eyes. She responded bluntly, "If there isn't better collaboration out of this group, changes will be made… and I'm not just talking severances. They've been looking to siphon our department into other services lines for months." Sandra let the information register before continuing, "I won't let you all continue to silo off into angry cliques. Forget downsizing and budget cut, the first thing to slip when everybody bickers is safety. Do you want to be responsible for a serious incident that will bury this hospital in a lawsuit?" Sandra let the information sink in. As she walked away, she realized that she might be reprimanded for speaking that way in front of a physician — yet another thing to worry about at night when she was supposed to be sleeping.

Sandra and the Endocrinology Department had been receiving considerable administrative pressure partly because other teams at the hospital were thriving. The hospital's Cardiovascular

Department was the most profitable service line. The integrated team of cardiologists, surgeons, administrators, nurses, and other specialties worked together like a well-oiled machine. The entire team didn't seem to harbor any resentments and stayed focused on the work. Not all service lines at the hospital could be profitable, but if the Cardiovascular Department could work with such interdependent cohesion, other teams should be able to do the same.

Step 3. Analyzing Your Team – Finding the Right Fuel Mixture

Have Each Team Member Answer the Following Questions:

1. Are you motivated by competitive opportunities, or do you feel less motivated by them?
2. Do you prefer competing against others, or do you prefer competing within yourself?
3. Do you tend to be more motivated by external reinforcement, internal fulfillment, or a combination of both?
4. What's your level of motivation when collaborating with others? What do you find enjoyable and what do you find challenging when you collaborate with others?
5. Have you experienced more success in goal attainment in competitive situations or collaborative situations?
6. How have life experiences influenced your motivation for competitive or collaborative situations?
7. How have life experiences influenced the importance you place on outcomes?
8. What do you hope to accomplish in your work both short-term and long-term? Why? Categorize each goal you hope to accomplish in terms of wants, values, or needs. Wants = an interest or desire; Values = an important source of fulfillment and meaning; Needs = essential to my self-esteem.
9. At this time in your life, what value do you prioritize higher: Independence – autonomy and self-reliance, or Interdependence – understanding and attending to the expectations of others? What influenced the development of that prioritization? How does that value impact your perspective on competition and collaboration in your organization?

Collect responses from everyone and analyze the blend of motivational influences. Create three continuums and plot individuals according to the following anchors: Collaborative to Competitive motivation; Process to Outcome motivation; and Independent to Interdependent values. The collaborative-competitive continuum should be plotted based on being strongly motivated by collaboration; relatively motivated by both; or strongly motivated by collaboration. The process-outcome continuum should be plotted based on being strongly motivated by outcomes; relatively motivated between the two; or strongly motivated by collaboration. The independent-interdependent continuum should be plotted based on being strongly motivated by independence; relatively balanced motivation between the two; or strongly motivated by interdependence. Once this is plotted, review with the team and provide an opportunity for them to make changes on the graph.

Step 4. Readying for &: Motivation as a Marathon, not a Sprint

Finding the right balance of sustainable motivation is challenging but absolutely doable if you assess a team's makeup as it pertains to competition, collaboration, process, outcome, independence, and interdependence. From that data, tailored goals and performance markers can be established for individuals along the continuums.

From Wants to Values to Goals

Moving individuals to a clarification of what is truly motivational can begin with a question that can seem egocentric, "What do you want from this experience?" We are naturally guided by our most important wants and values, but it's often hard to talk about them without feeling overly self-focused. If an organization gives voice to this line of thought, it sends the message that this is important enough for everyone to give it some time and reflection. "What do you want?" is a good starting point because it invites reflection on something of natural personal interest.

Using each person's stated want, have each individual engage in prioritizing those wants. Discuss in small groups the "why" behind each want and why the higher prioritized values are more important at this time in their lives. Through this process, an organization begins to develop a narrative describing these highly important wants as motivational values. Keep the list small, keep distinguishing between wants that are preferences without motivational commitment and wants that are so important they create sustainable drive.

Goals can be developed from each person's most prized motivational values. Patterns will often emerge among those goals across individuals. Some will have wants that will be comparative with others; some will have goals that are competitive within themselves; and some goals will be more interdependent and collaborative. From the team analysis data, break the team into smaller groups that reflect a shared point on the continuum to discuss the individual goals that are emerging. This allows people of similar approaches to support, affirm, and edit goals without feeling like they have to defend why their wants are prioritized the way they are. Then have them meet with team members that are on different points on the continuum so that a sense of understanding and respect for individual differences can be developed. The key component of this process is that if the goals are reasonable and healthy (which is facilitated by discussing them with others), they should be honored because they matter to individuals and because they tap into a more intrinsic level of motivation. This brings up the issue of intrinsic versus extrinsic motivation as it pertains to goal setting.

So much analysis in the social sciences has been applied to check whether intrinsic motivation − being motivated by internal factors, such as values − or extrinsic motivation − being motivated by external factors, such as monetary reward − is optimal for sustained motivation. In our work with organizations, we have found that it is rarely that simple or dichotomized. At the ends of the continuum, yes, it is clear that someone who is only motivated by extrinsic factors will experience less motivation when those external factors are removed. And on the other end of the continuum, a person who is primarily motivated by intrinsic factors will also find it challenging to sustain motivation when they are in a chronically inequitable environment where there is not a fair recognition of one's talents and efforts. It is important to respect a blending of both intrinsic and extrinsic forms of motivation by understanding what those motivations may look like for each individual. Bringing a higher sense of regard for each individual can also increase sustainable motivation (Blanchard, 1985; Drucker, 1954; Hersey & Blanchard, 1988; Locke, 1990; Smith & Chadwick, 1999).

Performance Psychology Tips for Sustainable Motivation

Goals without equity impact trust. Goals without trust impact morale, performance, and retention. This chapter has focused on how to create a culture of sustained motivation by recognizing varying fuels of motivation across individuals. But what is recognized and rewarded in an organization? If an organization is inclusive of varying levels of motivation, it needs to incorporate equitable and variable forms of recognition and reward. A university that promotes wellness and developing wellness goals, but only rewards and recognizes those students who are the highest achievers will only serve to create a culture of stress glorification, not wellness. Organizations need to make sure that as goals are developed, there are linear connections of those goals to reward and recognition structures within an organization, even for those individuals who are primarily motivated by intrinsic factors. For some, recognition and reward are primary motivators, for others, it's seen as a bonus to the work they already find meaningful. Seeing equity in action plays an important role in establishing and preserving morale, trust, and ultimately, retention.

Goal development helps with supervision but never replaces it. The cornerstone of this approach assumes an invitation for the development of healthy, reasonable goals. The **invitation** for healthy goal development is necessary, but not always sufficient. When people are unhealthy, it is challenging to develop healthy goals. So, supervision is still necessary to ensure that healthy goals are developmentally moving someone forward. The process recommended in this chapter creates an organizational dynamic that includes peer discussion and feedback, which can help with the supervisory process of finalizing goals. Supervision also provides the opportunity for linking individual goals to the overarching organizational mission and vision. The focus is not only on the individual, it is finding a deeper source of motivation that is individualized so that each person can tap into their why and be committed to their work for the organization. Sometimes this process is smooth, other times it is quite difficult because of personal issues that may be impacting the lens of how they see themselves and the organization. Regular supervisory meetings can help detect when there is a healthy perspective and when that perspective is strained.

Don't let wisdom replace smartness. While it isn't sexy or provocative, goals that incorporate both competition and collaboration should still not stray too far from the basics of solid goal development. In other words, don't stray too far from SMART goals (Doran, 1981; Morrison, 2010). As individuals move from their wants to their values to crystallizing how those look in their goals, encourage them to make sure their goals are specific, measureable, achievable, relevant, and timely.

Cooperation is not collaboration. It is very easy for people to confuse cooperation with collaboration. "Sure, I'll help you out." "How can I support you in your work?" "I'm a team player." "I work well with others." These are all phrases that are cooperative. The key difference between cooperation and collaboration is shared responsibility. Cooperation takes the form of, "I'm happy to help you with your work, but the responsibility for the project's success or failure is yours." Collaboration is stepping in and owning shared responsibility for a project even if you don't have positional leadership. You feel a sense of healthy stress about the project because you believe that you are a part of its success or failure. This is much harder and vulnerable because you are putting yourself out there to be evaluated. Cooperation is much easier because it safely allows you to step in and help while also allowing you to step out when being evaluated. It's important for organizations to have open conversations about the distinction between cooperation and collaboration. Be explicit about differentiating collaboration and cooperation (e.g., "I'm fine with taking on the sole responsibility of the project but I need a little help with a couple of specific pieces of the work.")

The best mindset for challenging performance goals. There are times when goals feel fully within one's capacity. Think of your emotions along a continuum of excited, nervous, and anxious when considering certain goals. When your confidence is high in your abilities and you believe the outcome is confidently attainable, you may feel excited as you start performing toward that goal. However, when our confidence in our abilities is high but the outcomes are uncertain, we may feel nervous before we perform, but nervousness does not have to be considered a negative emotion. When our confidence in our abilities is shaky and the outcomes are uncertain, we tend to feel anxious before we perform, which tends to negatively impact both motivation and performance. So, what do we do when we know a goal is going to require a lot from us with no guarantees? We must be aware that goals which require a lot from us also require commitment to a certain mindset when stepping into a performance. A mindset that focuses on (1) positioning goals and (2) a specific view on outcomes.

No matter the different forms of motivation that exist within an organization, at the moment of performance, individuals should focus their performance on goals that are within their control. Anything else is a distraction and affects a person's perceived capabilities compared to the perceived demands. That is done by developing *positioning goals*. Positioning goals are goals that are within a person's control that best position them to attain the desired outcome. This is especially important with challenging outcomes. The best way to develop positioning goals is to start with a desired outcome (e.g., an A in class, a first place finish in an athletic competition, attaining grant funding). Then list as many factors as possible that have to occur to get that outcome. Review all of the factors and draw a line through any factors that are not within your control. What is left over are positioning goals that are within your control and best position you to attain that outcome. During a performance, any focus on the factors that were crossed off, only serve to impair performance.

Our mindset about outcomes at the moment of performance matters, too. We all know that outcomes are important. Our body will respond to truth but it won't respond to mind games. Trying to convince ourselves that outcomes don't matter only serves to create an argument in our head because we know that they do matter. Outcomes serve five positive purposes: (1) they can serve as an additional motivation to do something we find hard, unpleasant, or boring; (2) they serve as a reward for our hard work; (3) they provide feedback about our work; (4) they can create expanded opportunities for us in the future; and (5) we tend to feel positively evaluated by others when we attain outcomes. So, outcomes matter. It's okay to want positive outcomes. And as long as outcomes remain a "want to" in our mental approach, they work for us. However, when outcomes shift from a "want to" to a "have to," they significantly get in the way of our optimal performance. If I have to have an outcome, then I cannot fail. If I cannot fail, then my fear of failure exponentially increases and I can slip into over-control or avoidance mode resulting in a plateau effect.

How do we keep outcomes in perspective amidst the pressure of needing outcomes to succeed in life? The key is to move from a noun focus to a verb focus. Nouns are outcomes (e.g., grades, achievements, relationships), which we don't completely control. When we have the mindset of needing outcomes, we are very noun-focused. By contrast, verbs are what we do. They are our actions, which we have more control over. When we don't control something, we become more aware of uncertainty, which can increase fear. A verb focus keeps fear in perspective because it concentrates our energy and attention on our behavior instead factors beyond our control.

In fact, you can limit your focus to just four verbs each day when you're stepping into a challenging performance: *learning, expressing what you've learned, relating, and taking care of yourself.* At any given time of the day, one of these fours verbs will be relevant. When you study, study to learn not for grades. When it's time to take a test focus on expressing what you've learned. When interacting with others, focus on how you want to relate with the other person (e.g., with kindness, curiosity, or respect). When we focus on the relationship instead of relating, we become very evaluative and constantly read how the other person is reacting to us. Concentrating on the verb of relating is one of the skills people with social anxiety use to interact more effectively with others despite feeling uncomfortable. And anytime during the day when you're not learning, expressing what you've learned, or relating, focus on taking care of yourself. Whenever you find yourself overwhelmed by nouns and outcomes, take a deep breath, and move into the most applicable verb.

There are several advantages to being verb-focused. First, it keeps fear in its proper perspective. Second, the more verb-focused you are, the more nouns you collect. You actually attain more outcomes because you're in an optimal mindset for high performance. There's a popular mantra about the importance of focusing on process versus outcome for high performance. That's partly true. It's not just process, though; it has to be purposeful process. You must be engaged in a process that has true purpose and relevance for you in order to perform at your highest level. A third advantage is that hard work is more acceptable when you're verb-focused. When you're staying within yourself and engaged in purposeful work, you are more accepting of the hardness and stress that comes with it. When we're focused on nouns, we become overwhelmed with everything we have to control to get the outcomes. The difficulty of all we have to attend to and manage becomes less acceptable. Fourth, and most important, when we are verb-focused, we experience more joy when we actually attain outcomes. When we have to have an outcome and are noun-focused the first emotion we experience when we attain that outcome is not joy, it's relief. When we are verb-focused, the success is in the work and outcomes are viewed as a bonus — icing on the cake. Remember, there is nothing wrong with wanting an outcome, it's needing it that gets in our way (Crace & Crace, 2020).

Step 5. Giving Voice to &: From Game Plan to Action to Maximizing Sustainable Motivation

How did the Stallions establish a platform for both Competition and Collaboration during a disappointing season?

While drawing what looked to be a field diagram, but it wasn't of a soccer field, Kat asked the group that had now settled into silence, "Any of y'all know how to play cricket?" She continued to draw and outline of a cricket pitch. "So this is the bowling crease. The bowler is like a pitcher and they throw it at the wickets which are protected by a batsman. . ." Kat continued to draw and explain the game of cricket. The players looked around questioning the mental stability of their coach.

Eventually, one of the assistant coaches interrupted Kat, "Excuse me, coach. We're due back on the field soon."

"Ok." Kat capped the dry erase marker and asked, "Robyn. What do you want out of this season?"

Robyn, surprised at being addressed, said, "A win."

"More selfishly," Kat challenged.

"Better stats. More goals."

"More selfish."

"I don't know." Robyn looked at the veteran she had fought and allowed herself to respond honestly, "I don't want washed-up jerks like her to screw up my career." Robyn stood up, "I don't want everyone to keep phoning it in this season. I don't want this team to ruin my career before it even starts."

"Ok." Kat looked at the veteran. "What do you want?"

"For little brats not to fight me in the locker room."

Kat repeated, "What do you want?"

The veteran let her anger drop and stated with simple, palpable honesty, "To keep playing."

Kat clapped her hands, "Alright. After this atrocity of a match, I want each of you to spend the evening writing out an email explaining your most selfish wants, goals, interests, expectations, expressions, whatever. Tell me what you want out of this season — for yourself." She waited till the instruction registered with the team, "Now get out there and finish this awful game so we can start cleaning up this mess."

The emails from players varied. Many players were concerned about maximizing their career earnings, which required enough opportunities to demonstrate their abilities for scouts and GMs. Other players simply wanted more playing time. Many older players wanted to play at the professional level for as long as they could.

Some wrote out more nuanced goals like wanting to recover from injuries carefully rather than rush back to competition too quickly. Some wanted traded to other teams. And a few wanted to try playing other positions that they felt could showcase more of their talents.

As the players suited up for morning drills, Kat entered the locker room. "Everybody put your street clothes back on, we're going for brunch. No training today."

Kat had rented out a catered banquet hall at a local hotel. As the players finished their brunch, Kat and the assistant coaches wheeled in large pinup boards with an aggregate of the 'wants' she had comprised from the team's emails. "Alright folks, all of you were pretty honest about what you're looking to get out of the rest of this season. The encouraging thing is that most of you didn't mention outcomes like win-loss records or specific stats. You all mostly want to have an opportunity to play the way you feel is best for you." She paused to make sure everybody was listening, "This is possible, but it's going to take collaboration. The goal here is to come up with a plan that will allow everybody a chance to go after what matters most to them." She turned to the boards joking, "It might be a disaster, but what have we got to lose?"

Kat unveiled different pinup boards in different areas in the room. "Ok, if More Playing Time is your prioritized Want, go to this section of the room." Several players went to that area of the room. "If your goal is to properly heal, rest, or recover this season, stay seated. We don't want you pulling a hammy at a team meeting."

Kat went on arranging the players into different sections, which took some discussion, "Renna, you already have a ton of playing time. Why are you standing in the More Playing Time section?"

"I want a bigger contract."

"What do you need to do to get that bigger contract?"

"More goals."

"Ok go stand in the Change Positions and Schemes group." After Renna and a dozen other players adjusted to different groups, Kat addressed everybody. "Ok, winning and strict outcomes are out the window. Convention is out the window. I'm not going to organize the team in a way that gives us the best chance to win," Kat said the cliché in a mocking tone.

"From now on, all decisions from positions, to playing time, to game strategy, to rest, travel, practice, everything... All decisions from now on will be based on allowing each player an opportunity to play for some of their highest prioritized wants, or values for short."

After some skeptical nodding, Kat went around the room and had each individual player express what they wanted and what that would look like in the context of the next match. By the time every player had spoken and Kat had listed that expression on the dry erase board, she took a step back and then addressed the team, "You can see its impossible for all of you to do everything in this next game. So for each of you to have an opportunity, it means each of you are going to have to give up a little to allow other teammates their opportunity."

Kat then went around the room bartering with players about what they were willing to give up. After two hours an assistant coach noticed the entire mood and interaction between the players had shifted. They still hadn't come up with a finalized plan, but players were sitting next to each other; joking at times; and brainstorming strategy ideas instead of arguing.

For many of the players time had gone by quickly when Kat abruptly stopped the meeting, "Ok. It's not perfect, but it's a good start. The coaches and I will come up with a game plan that tries to accommodate...," she jokingly pointed to the graffitied dry erase board, "this mess. And next week we'll do another brunch meeting just like this and try again."

Reporters and fans didn't know what to think about the Stallions new strategy. Kat was subbing in players every 15 minutes, changing player formations constantly, listing way too many players on the injured reserve list, and assigning players to positions they had never played before.

Week after week, they held a brunch and ironed out a new plan. Every player would get a chance to express their values, how that could be applied to the next game, and what they didn't like about last game's strategy.

Kat received criticism and mockery from fans and reporters. But week after week the cohesion, resilience, and overall mood of the team had clearly improved. The Stallions were no longer getting blown out and after a couple of draws and an actual victory even the most critical fans were talking about the team's turn around.

By the end of the season, the Stallions almost snuck into the last playoff spot. When they didn't and the season ended, Kat arranged one last brunch meeting. "Alright, I want to hear each person's assessment of the season as far as their Wants or Values, whatever term you like best."

A few players expressed gratitude for more playing time. Others appreciated more time to rest and recover from physical and mental challenges. A few team members said they learned more about their strengths as players by being able to play different positions and formations. Robyn had even been offered a contract for next season with one of the league's best teams.

One of the veteran players said, "I don't think I achieved many of the Wants that I thought I wanted. But this has been one of the most interesting if not fun seasons I've ever had playing in the league. It's given me a new lease on motivation going into the offseason. I just want to keep playing." She thought through her thoughts and continued sharing, "Every offseason I dread training cause I never know if it will be enough for a team to pick me up next season. It's agonizing. But this season has given me something — a looseness, a flow with the game. We all competed together — for each other. I feel stronger... ya know?"

As other team members shared their assessments, one player asked Kat, "What was your Want for this season."

Kat smirked and said, "This," she motioned around the room. "Y'all probably know about my injury at the Olympics when I was a player. Well after a solid five years of reeling and self-destruction, I found a job in New Zealand so I could move as far away from everything I knew." She sat down in a chair amongst the players, "Long story, short. I fell in love with cricket out there. My knee held up enough for me to play in a little semi-pro circuit and I had a coach who used this coaching style." Kat shrugged her shoulders and laughed, "I wanted to try out that coaching style here. So when y'all were falling apart, I got in touch with the owner, told her about this system." She looked at the veteran player, "I promised her the system would turn the team around and we'd make the playoffs." She laughed to herself. "We almost did." Robyn shouted.

"I didn't think we'd make the playoffs. I just wanted to implement a system of motivation that would last ... And we did."

How did Sandra and the Endocrinology Department find a way to embrace both Independence and Interdependence?

Sandra scheduled a meeting with Dr. Waltrip and shared the pressures and concerns she was feeling around team motivation and morale. She proposed having an informal meeting with their counterparts in Cardio over dinner to learn what they have been doing to manage the same administrative pressures. In a moment of brief vulnerability, Dr. Waltrip shared his concern about the team and even though that was often expressed as frustration and anger, he found himself more worried than angry at the end of the day.

At dinner with their colleagues from Cardio, Shawn and Dr. Stelljes, Sandra discussed the pattern that the department had fallen into and how it was starting to impact the group. Both her and Dr. Waltrip acknowledged something different about the Cardio team and wanted to learn more about what they were doing differently.

Dr. Stelljes smiled and said, "You can't laugh, okay?"

Shawn nodded at Sandra, "This is a good story."

"And it's true," Dr. Stelljes confirmed. "So, I was playing a charity golf tournament for my daughter's high school. One of the guys that was in my foursome used to be an Assistant Coach for the US Olympic Men's Team Handball Team. I didn't know much about the sport, and since we were in the cart together all day, I started asking questions like, how did he keep the team motivated when playing in a country where Handball isn't popular? And the coach ended up relating that challenge back to the larger team challenges that they always had to effectively manage. And as he was describing those dynamics, the more parallels I was seeing with our team in Cardio — strong vertical hierarchy, lots of talent, lots of intelligence, lots of egos, and lots of power differential. So, I gave up on my focus on golf and just became a sponge, soaking up everything he had to offer.

"One of the most helpful things he discussed was establishing personal goals in the context of team. He talked about the differences he would notice every year in terms of what motivated each person. Some were highly competitive, some were more focused internally and staying within themselves to measure success, some were very team-oriented, some were process-oriented while others were outcome-focused, and some were fiercely independent, while others always looked to others for input. He talked about creating space for all of those perspectives instead of trying to impose a culture that only rewarded one or two types of motivation. He kept talking about diversity being a strong predictor of flourishing, rather than trying to select players that had the same orientation, experiences, and perspectives. He said the reason it worked is that it got at what was most important to each individual in terms of motivation and reward, while simultaneously gaining an understanding and appreciation of how others are motivated. He walked me through their goal setting process: the right questions to ask to get the right information from the individuals and then how to make sense of it as collective. I took it back to Shawn and she agreed to help me with the process. It was clumsy at first but we just stayed with it and struggled through together."

Shawn added, "But to be honest, the real turning point was when we," she motioned to Dr. Stelljes and herself, "put our egos aside and honestly acknowledged that we had been using a hierarchical system for our benefit, not for the team."

Dr. Stelljes agreed, "I know that all hospitals have to have a hierarchy to some degree, but when it comes down to smaller teams and departments, all individuals need to feel seen, heard, and valued, not just the ones at the top of the ladder."

Dr. Waltrip felt his face getting warm and flushed. This comment struck a personal note with him and he couldn't hide his physical response. He immediately got quiet, played with his food, and retreated into his memories. He hated being questioned and criticized so openly by nurses. And he knew why — he just didn't like to be reminded of it. One of the reasons that medicine appealed to him was the status, privilege, and hierarchy of medicine. He had never felt the respect of his family. Nothing he did growing up was good enough. He was constantly criticized. The only out he had was his intelligence and his natural proclivity to science. He loved science, and he did honestly find great meaning in helping others; but as a young man with even younger maturity, a strong motivator that pushed him through medical school was that others would have to defer to what he said and did. He was sensitive to criticism, and he never had a mentor that was able to provide a corrective experience; so the sensitivity remained and any form of negative or critical feedback was met with immediate rejection and defensiveness. Power would quickly take over and usually ended with "because I said so."

"John, wouldn't you agree?" his colleague asked.

"I'm sorry, I drifted away for a minute. Agree about what?"

"That so much of our training and culture is about hierarchy, and while it's understandable at some level, is it as necessary at the extremes that we take it?"

"I guess, it's just all that I've known, and it worked for me... until now, when it feels like I'm criticized for everything I do by the nurses. It frankly pisses me off."

"It did me, too," replied Dr. Stelljes. "But it wasn't until I truly looked at why they weren't working well as a team and realizing that my attitude was playing a part in it. Ironically, when we went to this new approach, and got through the clumsy learning curve of it, I realized that I was being treated with a lot more respect than when I was relying on my position to demand it.

Listen, I know this is hard to consider, it goes against all of our training, but, at some level, you know that something has to change, otherwise you wouldn't have had the courage to reach out to us. That says something very positive about how important this team is to you and to Sandra. Let that be the starting point."

The next day, Sandra and Dr. Waltrip spent their Saturday in the office mapping out the questions they would lead the team through on Monday. They reached out to the team asking them to adjust their schedules to plan on meeting for a two-hour catered dinner on Monday evening to do some team development. At the end of their planning meeting, Sandra expressed appreciation for Dr. Waltrip's openness to dive into this work. As she left, Dr. Waltrip said, "Sandra, it's John, call me John."

References

Blanchard, K. (1985). *Leadership and the one-minute manager.* HarperCollins.

Brown, B. (2018). *Dare to lead: Brave work. Tough conversations. Whole hearts.* Penguin Random House.

Crace, R.K., & Crace, R.L. (2020). *Authentic Excellence: Flourishing and resilience in a relentless world.* Routledge.

Doran, G.T. (1981). There's a S.M.A.R.T. way to write management's goals and objectives. *Management Review, 70,* 35.

Drucker, P. (1954). *The practice of management.* HarperCollins.

Hersey, P.H., & Blanchard, K. (1988). *Management of organizational behavior.* Prentice-Hall, Inc.

Locke, E.A., & Latham, G.P. (1990). *A theory of goal setting and task performance.* Prentice-Hall, Inc.

Morrison, M. (2010). *History of SMART objectives.* Rapid Business Improvement. http://rapidbi.com/management/history-of-smart-objectives/

Smith, D., & Chadwick, D. (1999). *The twelve leadership principles of Dean Smith.* Total/Sports Illustrated.

4

STRESSED "&" WELL

TRANSFORMATIVE OPTIMIZER: RESILIENCE

Jessica hadn't expected the business to take off like it did. Now eight months after launching her tech startup, the honeymoon was over.

She had a small team of 12 employees and though Jessica was younger than most of her staff, she'd done a commendable job keeping team stress at a minimum. But now Jessica could sense tensions arising among team members. Tensions that if not managed effectively, could possibly derail the progress made in this start-up phase. Jessica wasn't exactly sure how to deal with the mounting tension and was beginning to feel more and more stress about the sustainability of her organization.

Sheila joined Jessica's startup earlier that year; she was encouraged by the company's attention to wellness and mental health. There were quarterly retreats; accommodated schedule adjustments when Sheila had issues with childcare; and weekly group meetings designated for openly airing any grievances or stressors team members were experiencing.

After six months of working at the startup, Sheila began to feel like she was languishing. She wanted more of a push for herself and more urgency

DOI: 10.4324/9781003265726-4

in her teammates. Certain initiatives like restructuring hiring practices and researching different healthcare plans were avoided because Jessica and other team members didn't want to delve into projects that could create a stressful environment.

Tom felt the company was too stressful. He had a family. He was taking night courses for advanced tech certifications. He also had to take care of his parents who were experiencing more health concerns as they aged. The administrative work required of Tom at the company was barely manageable and increasing each week.

At weekly meetings, Sheila started advocating that the group take on more difficult projects. "I feel like we have the resources to create more accessible systems in the way we do things here."

Tom struggled to stave off his anxiety every time Sheila made a proactive suggestion. Why was she rocking the boat with these over-achieving initiatives? They wouldn't be getting paid more to work on these projects. Tom's anxiety progressively turned to anger each time Sheila brought up another ambitious project.

When Sheila discussed different ideas at the weekly meetings, the reaction from the team ranged from polite avoidance to desperate dismissal. Why was she working at a place that didn't want to improve the accessibility and efficiency of their operations? In her mind, the company simply needed to commit to raising the bar. While wellness was important, Sheila was OK with focusing on the pursuit of inclusion and excellence rather than wellness. To her, if the business was going to succeed, it was becoming clear, the team could focus on Stress OR Wellness, not both!

Step 1. Recognizing the OR Conflict: The Branding of Stress as Unwell

Today's organizational leaders are more sophisticated in understanding the factors that impact recruitment and retention. Issues like quality of benefits, wellbeing, and work-life considerations are important in sustaining a healthy work culture. With greater emphasis placed on wellness, stress can be characterized as unhealthy or counterproductive to a healthy work environment. Stress is often portrayed as an impediment to wellness. Other attitudes around stress have painted wellness and self-care as "throttling back" to the point of compromising high performance. When we consider stress with pre-determined connotations, we can miss out on healthy aspects associated with stress and become less aware of how stress may be impacting other individuals in our organizations. Sheila felt like the concept of wellness was being used as a rationale for not focusing on important organizational initiatives. She felt a culture had been created to where wellness was equated with non-stress. Organizational members can feel like they too have to choose between the stress of productivity "Or" the prioritization of their wellbeing. Even within the same company, Tom was experiencing a collective push to do more while Sheila was feeling like the norm was to avoid discomfort.

"Or" cultures can be created when fear and need start to lead, causing over-attention to one team dynamic over the other. Sheila started worrying about the impact of the organization not spending time on issues she felt were critical. What started out to be a culture that was appealing to her gradually became a source of concern and worry. Tom, on the other hand, was becoming increasingly concerned and worried about anything else being added to his plate due to the overwhelming demands he was managing. Jessica could intuit the tension but was hesitant to address a potentially stressful conflict. She wasn't confident that if she did summon the energy to address the tension that the company would find any sort of resolution further distracting the company from working on important issues like restructuring hiring practices.

The side of the Or an organization leans toward depends a lot on power and numbers – how much cultural traction a particular dynamic has among members of the organization. But what if stress was an essential component of a healthy work culture? What if stress and wellness could work in concert to fuel authentic excellence for the organization? More specifically, what if a culture of "&" was created that allowed for the integration of both dynamics. Rather than establishing a culture that managed the tension of the dynamics by selecting one OR the other, what if the organization developed a culture of managing the tension by focusing on both. This chapter deconstructs stress and demonstrates how a focus on stress management versus stress reduction can elevate an organization to a higher level of resilience. This transformative optimizer of resilience allows the organization to employ flourishing strategies that are values-centered.

Step 2. Finding the Purpose of &: Stress Being Essential to Resilience

When an organization shifts from being fear-centered to values-centered, there is greater clarity on the integrative nature of stress and wellness. Stress is a function of importance. You can't feel stress about something that is unimportant. So if an organization creates a values-centered culture, there will be some stress associated with those values. For example, if an organization embraces the value of Responsibility, then there will be some stress associated with the "should" of being dependable and trustworthy with others. By embracing stress as an essential component of a work culture then it removes one of the biggest obstacles to wellness – perceiving stress as bad. Research indicates that stress does not increase our health risks, it's the perception that stress is bad that negatively impacts our health – thus it is your belief or mindset about the stress you experience that makes the difference (Crum & Crum, 2015; Crum, Salovey, & Achor, 2013; Forshaw & Sheffield, 2012; Jamieson, Nock, & Mendes, 2012; Johnston, 1993; Keller et al., 2012; Lazarus & Folkman, 1984; McGonigal, 2015).

So, perception of stress matters. In addition, perception of ourselves in stress matters. Stress is not only a function of importance, but is also a function of the inverse relationship between perceived demands and perceived capabilities. If we perceive our demands to exceed our capabilities, we're stressed. If we perceive our capabilities to exceed our demands, we're bored, which can also be perceived as stressful. The key is to find the right balance of perceived capabilities and demands. The critical word is *perceived*. The more demands and weight of those demands that we carry, the less capable and confident we feel. Consider the many demands that we place on ourselves that don't have to be demands – the demand of needing a certain outcome to feel successful, the demand for everyone's approval, the demand to be perfect, to be the best.

Organizations that can embrace the stress associated with their values and goals while managing the balance of perceived capabilities and perceived demands can withstand tremendous stress and thereby increasing resilience. Perceiving wellness as a state of calm or a lack of stress sets one up for perceiving stress as a crisis, which can leave individuals vulnerable to burnout over time. These misperceptions negatively impact resilience because they distort its meaning. Resilience is often mistakenly viewed as not being impacted or affected by stressful or difficult circumstances. Resilience is actually having the ability to manage difficult emotions and circumstances in a healthy manner – even while affected. When stress & wellness are seen as equally healthy and essential, then a deeper sense of resilience is created because purpose and meaning are the leading motivators rather than calm or happiness. The key to this higher order of resilience is to (1) elevate both stress and health as essential, (2) see both as being a part of engaging in values-centered behavior, and (3) build a confidence among team members to manage stress in a healthy manner. Thus, the key to integrating stress and wellness is the activation of higher orders of resilience. Activation of this type of resilience serves as the transformative optimizer to give voice to the & culture that leads to organizational flourishing.

What if Sheila appealed to the organizational values as a way of discussing the importance of some of the projects she was advocating for? What if Tom viewed stress as a function of importance and recognized that all of the stressful things on his plate were all related to efforts that really mattered to him and that the feelings represented natural consequences of inclusion and excellence? Could it provide more mental space for him to consider other values-laden initiatives? What if all members of the organization weighed in on integration of the singular dynamics? Solutions could be discovered that create a culture of &. Fear, need, and power would give way to values-based decision-making propelling the organization to authentic excellence.

Step 3. Analyzing Your Team: The Appearance of Stress & Wellness in Your Organization

Understanding Stress in your Organization

What does stress look like in your organization? What would you estimate to be the major sources of stress of your colleagues? Who are the primary drivers of stress in your organization?

What are the rationalizations members of the organization are using to lock into a singular dynamic? What levers are available to employ that would move the group toward flourishing?

Consider the following types of stress that are prominent among members of your organization:

Stress Within Roles – Stress that occurs when important values within a certain role (work, relationships, leisure, etc.) are not being fulfilled or respected. The environment or people in authority may be preventing individuals from fulfilling their values or are demanding that time and energy on other values.

Stress Between Roles – Stress that occurs when time and energy on one life role is interfering with time devoted to roles where other values are being fulfilled.

Stress of Managing Too Many Values – Stress that occurs when managing too many values that feel critical but are unable to attend to most of them particularly well. Most life role configurations combined with available time and energy do not permit people to satisfy a large number of values.

Internal Conflict – At times our values can be contradictory and cause ambivalence. For instance, someone who values Belonging and Independence will have to manage the stress of attending to both differing values. Unresolved emotions from difficult life experiences may also interfere with values fulfillment. For example, unresolved fear of failure can interfere with Achievement; or, unresolved hurt from broken trust can interfere with Belonging. Feeling incapable of acting on values that are important to us can be a sign that our typical methods of coping and support are not enough to work through an important conflict.

Unresolved emotional issues can also cause values to drift into intense needs. When a value becomes a need, the fulfillment we feel from expressing that value starts to be replaced with stress and intensity. This is because we are over-attending to that need at the expense of other important values. For example, if we value Responsibility we will be motivated to be dependable and trustworthy. But *needing* to be responsible is overwhelming because we have to be seen as dependable to everyone in all situations, a need that can never be completely satisfied. We will live in fear of letting others down, and can become stressed to the point where we have no energy for other values. Eventually, the need to be responsible to others results in less responsibility to your own health. When there are enough people in an organization who are managing internal conflicts, it can create a culture that depicts stress as problematic and emotional calm becomes the driver of decisions.

How is health or wellness described in your organization? Is it defined in a very limited manner, such as physical or emotional health; or is defined more holistically and multi-dimensional? Who are the primary drivers of how wellness is perceived in your organization?

Understanding Health & Wellness in your Organization

How is wellness defined in your organization? What is the dialogue about wellness and what policies, procedures, practices, and traditions would be congruent with wellness?

Consider the following dimensions of wellness from the National Wellness Institute. What level of importance, priority, time, and attention does your organization give to these dimensions of wellness?

The 8 Dimensions of Wellness

- Emotional/Mental – Coping effectively, having a sense of positive self-regard, and creating meaningful relationships.
- Environmental – Creating pleasant, stimulating environments that support wellbeing.
- Financial – Feeling healthy, confident, and informed about current and future financial issues.
- Intellectual – Being engaged in activities that expand knowledge and skills that are intellectually stimulating.
- Occupational – Personal satisfaction and enrichment from one's work.
- Physical – Engaged in healthy physical activity, having a healthy relationship with food, and engaged in restorative rest and sleep.
- Social – Developing a sense of connection, belonging, and a well-developed support system.
- Spiritual – Attending to our sense of purpose and meaning in life.

How is wellness defined in your organization? What is the dialogue about wellness and what policies, procedures, practices, and traditions would be congruent with wellness?

At a recent staff meeting, Jessica invited the team to talk about stress and wellness. Using the framework of stress and wellness described above, she asked each team member to identify what their stress looks like and what wellness looks like for them. She then split the group up into pairs and asked them to share their answers with each other. Both Tom and Sheila felt apprehension when they were paired together.

Sheila shared that a large part of her stress was within her work role. One of the reasons she liked working for the company was their emphasis on wellness but lately she was experiencing a focus on wellness to the neglect of other important matters. She felt stress because she felt alone in this concern, which made her feel devalued. Sheila also recognized that this touched on personal issues of how she managed the frustration of blocked values such as Achievement and Responsibility. Coming from a patriarchal family of origin and working in industries that were equally patriarchal and sometimes misogynistic, she had developed a pattern of internalizing conflict and following the normative behavior at the cost of her health as evidenced by her chronic management of IBS. She also recognized that she had been neglecting several important dimensions of wellness that helped her cope with stress in a healthy manner. She loved taking early morning walks, which fulfilled her physical, emotional, and spiritual dimensions of wellness. She couldn't remember the last time she had taken a walk. She also loved boxing but hadn't been to her gym in several months. She laughed at the irony that she joined an organization because of their focus on wellness, and yet, she had become more distant from her wellness.

As Tom listened to Sheila, he found himself more interested than frustrated by what she was sharing. He better understood why these issues were important to her and the impact that it was having on her by not getting anyone to engage in the conversation. Tom shared with Sheila that his biggest source of stress was between roles because of all the juggling he was doing among his family, night classes, and his job. She immediately commiserated with the challenges of parenthood and education. She had been there. Tom shared that his biggest takeaway from the exercise was that stress was a function of importance. He realized that the demands in his life were not imposed on him; he had chosen all of them. And they all were important to him. If anyone tried to take one of those endeavors away, he would fight to keep it. But he also realized that he had completely neglected his wellness along the way. He was purely in survival mode.

The group came back together to share their discussions. It became clear to Jessica that there was quite a range of experiences as it related to perceived stress. Some staff members were overwhelmed while some wanted to be more challenged. Many expressed having not thought of stress as a positive feeling attached to their values. They were intrigued by the idea and felt it could make a difference in how the organization found the right balance between support and challenge. As a group, they decided to spend a little time during their weekly staff meetings exploring ways to better integrate healthy stress, effective coping, and wellness practices into their work culture. While not the answer to all the organization's challenges, the group had taken an important step in the pursuit of authentic excellence — acknowledging the & perspective to move the organization forward.

Step 4. Readying for &: Holding Stress Well

Once stress and wellness are better understood within a team, a game plan needs to be developed based on flourishing strategies that can optimize stress management and wellness.

Helping a Team Manage Stress

Matching stress management strategies to the type of stress experienced is important in creating a culture that can hold stress well. Team members who are experiencing **stress within roles** need to redefine responsibilities in that role; develop other activities that will compensate and allow for the values to be satisfied; or consider leaving that environment. Team members who are experiencing **stress between roles** need to reprioritize and align their time and energy according to their highest priority values. Team members who are experiencing the **stress of juggling too many values** need to reduce the list of critical values to a number that feels possible with their available time and energy (Crace & Crace, 2020).

For those who are managing the stress of an internal conflict, it may be helpful to encourage additional emotional support. It can feel scary and unsettling to recognize how patterns of unresolved internal conflicts can drift values into a need state and interfere with values expression. Devoting less time to a value that has drifted into a need-state can be overwhelming. The adjustment will feel wrong at first and may cause guilt. Organizations that can emphasize the concept of optimal expression versus maximum expression of values can help mediate that guilt. For example, if we have over-attended to the Responsibility value and believe it is healthy to devote less time to it, we may initially feel like we're being "irresponsible." Instead, we can view it as being *optimally* responsible.

Stress in the form of internal conflict can also be a psychological response to dealing with difficult emotions. In a group setting, when people are working hard on goals that have uncertain outcomes, difficult emotions of frustration, worry, hurt, anger, and guilt are bound to emerge. Often, effective stress and emotional management within a team depends less on what we do and more on the order in which we approach stress and difficult emotions. Following this filtering method of stress management can help a group gain greater confidence in managing difficult emotions.

This method of stress management is a process that is done individually but can be supported and reinforced at an organizational level.

1. **Acceptance – Seeing Stress as a Good Thing.** If the current stress is acceptable because it's connected to something that matters, go with it. Stress itself is not bad. It's a function of importance. It's impossible to be stressed about something that isn't important. Stress reduction can be misleading because it may require lowering the importance of something that matters. To be engaged in our values means we are also signing up for stress. This is a good thing... up to a point. There is an optimal point where we are engaged in our values but haven't moved them into a need state. For instance, we often go through crunch periods of absurd busyness. If we know that the stress stems from reasons of value and importance, and that the busyness is temporary, we are more likely to find an optimal level of acceptable stress. It is during these crunch times when we need to be more accepting, not evaluative or judgmental. It can also help to keep self-care practices in place even if we only have sparing moments to devote to self-care. The goal is stress management through acceptance not stress reduction.

2. **Problem-Solving.** If the stress level feels too high; explore whether there is something that can be done to fix or influence the situation. There might be a solution. Be analytical and reach out to others for their opinions. Develop a solution, a plan, and then engage in the process.

3. **Self-Imposed Pressure.** After problem-solving and action, if stress is still overwhelming, explore whether there may be self-imposed pressures or perceptions that add to the stress. Stress can be exasperated by our perceived demands and perceived capabilities. When our perceived demands exceed our perceived capabilities, we are stressed. At times our thoughts and demands add weight to our stress making it overwhelming, especially if our perceptions contain rigid "shoulds" or "needs." For example, "Life *should* be fair;" "There *should* be equitable return on my effort;" "We *need* to achieve this outcome to feel good about our work." Other forms of self-imposed pressure include over-projecting into the future; making broad conclusions; seeing everything as critically important; and trying to over-control as a way of managing fear. It is important for teams to identify prominent pressures and their

impact on team members. Motivational platitudes and clichés can often unintentionally create norms that interfere with performance because of unnecessary pressure. For example, "No pain, no gain," can create a culture that overlooks legitimate concerns and pressures which can cause team members to feel devalued." Again, stress is a good thing, up to a point, and an organization needs to understand what level of stress is motivational and when the stress begins to negatively affect performance. From that awareness, it is important for the team to collectively commit to catching those pressures when they emerge and turning the focus toward healthier behaviors and positive challenge. While the leader of the organization may feel this is his or her job, we believe this activity can be led by anyone on the team.

4. **Effective Coping**. If stress is still beyond an acceptable level after having attempted problem-solving and action steps, and after managing unnecessary self-imposed pressures; then the work is coping. To develop confidence in managing the harshness of our life experiences, people who flourish focus primarily on three essential steps for coping: (a) They honor their emotional reaction but challenge any conclusions they make about themselves and others while upset; (b) they develop healthy self-care strategies (e.g., verbal expression, physical expression, creative expression, meditative expression) instead of rushing to soothe just to feel better; and (c) they become very values focused, dedicating their energies toward things that matter most to them (Crace & Crace, 2020).

Team members can provide helpful support by reminding other members managing difficult emotions of these coping steps. But flourishing individuals and organizations intentionally work at developing their social support networks. People often think of social support as only emotional support, but social support can be considered more broadly to encompass eight dimensions (Hardy & Crace, 1993; Hardy, Burke, & Crace, 2005).

- Listening – Someone who actively listens without giving advice or being judgmental.
- Emotional Support – Someone you trust who provides comfort, care, and encouragement.
- Emotional Challenge – Someone who challenges you to examine your perspective, values, thoughts, and feelings.

- *Task Appreciation* – Someone who acknowledges your efforts and expresses appreciation for your work.
- *Task Challenge* – Someone who challenges the way you think about a task or activity that can lead to greater creativity, motivation, and involvement.
- *Reality Confirmation* – Someone who is coming from a similar reality or context helps confirm your perspective of the world.
- *Tangible Assistance* – Someone who provides financial assistance, products, and/or gifts.
- *Personal Assistance* – Someone who provides services or help through the contribution of their time and energy.

Teams that take the time to clarify the dimensions of social support and fill any gaps can create a culture that feels supportive and resilient against turmoil and difficult emotional experiences.

Helping a Team Develop Wellness Harmony

We often read and hear about the importance of work-life balance. The truth is that striving for work-life balance can get in the way of flourishing. It often can be too extreme of an expectation to devote a balanced level of energy and time to all of the things that matter to us. Therefore, when we strive to do so and fall short, we either end the day blaming ourselves for our failure to be balanced, or we blame the world for not allowing us to be balanced. The notion of work-life balance implies that life only exists outside of work when for most of us our work is an important part of our lives.

Organizations can have a better chance of flourishing if they think more in terms of harmony instead of balance. Each day brings new priorities, new challenges, and unexpected demands. If we start off each day asking, "What is the most right devotion of my time and energy today?" and follow that path, we will find that one day calls for full immersion into one endeavor, another day may involve many endeavors, and another day may be all about restoration. If we ask that question each day as if we have never asked it before, we can develop a flexible level of harmony in our life. A harmony and flexibility that is more centering than striving for balance. Understanding harmony in one's individual life contributes to practices that build a culture of & at the organizational level.

Approaching harmony as a centering practice also applies as a practice in wellness. Instead of thinking about wellness in a binary way, such as being sick or well, it can help to embrace a vision of integrative wellness — a multidimensional approach to thinking about wellness. Wellness can be viewed along a spectrum of 8 dimensions: Emotional, Environmental, Financial, Intellectual, Occupational, Physical, Social, & Spiritual.

To create a culture of wellness, teams can facilitate a more effective process of striving for harmony instead of balance. The Wellness Harmony exercise is a team practice where individuals develop their own harmony profile which also provides a springboard for discussion among team members. A deeper understanding of how wellness can be manifested and the "why" behind everyone's wellness profiles helps create a more authentic norm of a healthy work environment.

Team Exercise: Developing Your Harmony Profile

1. Reflect on the following 8 Dimensions of Wellness and clarify your own definition of what wellness looks like to you with each dimension: Emotional, Environmental, Financial, Intellectual, Occupational, Physical, Social, & Spiritual. What does it mean to you to be emotionally healthy and well? Ask that for each dimension.
2. Take a blank piece of paper and label that paper "My **Current** Harmony Profile." Graphically depict each dimension of wellness (using circles) based on two criteria: (a) How much time and energy are you devoting to that dimension? If you are devoting a lot of energy and time to that dimension, the circle should be large; if you are not, the circle should be small. (b) Importance. If a dimension of wellness is very important to you, draw the circle near the center of the page; if a dimension is not very important to you at this point in time, draw the circle near the edge of the page. If there are dimensions of wellness that interact with each other, make sure to draw those as overlapping circles.
3. Take a 2nd blank piece of paper and label that paper "My **Preferred** Harmony Profile." Repeat the same exercise as before but depict what you want your wellness harmony to look like. Keep in mind that you only have so much time in a day. You can't just increase the circle in all of your dimensions. If you increase the size of one circle, another circle will need to decrease.

4. Pick a time frame that you want to give yourself to move from your current harmony profile to the preferred harmony profile. You may pick Dec 31 as your goal, or three months from now. You pick the timeline that feels best for you.

5. Clarify the steps that need to occur to move to your preferred harmony profile. What facilitative factors are in place to help you move toward that profile, and what challenges may get in your way? What support and mentoring would be helpful for you (including any support you may want for specific dimensions)?

6. Share your answers from this exercise with a team member.

7. Return to the larger group and each team member will share an important takeaway that they appreciated from learning about their partner's wellness goals. Discuss common themes that emerge from the larger group discussion. Highlight facilitative organizational factors that facilitate wellness and factors that can restrict wellness. Spend time celebrating where a wellness culture is affirmed and brainstorm ways to attend to the restrictive factors.

Step 5. Giving Voice to &: From Game Plan to Action

Jessica added 30 minutes to the weekly staff meeting over the next quarter to be solely devoted to the tension between stress and wellness.

The first discussion centered on Worthwhile Stress. They talked as a group about what really mattered to them in their work and the consequential stress that stemmed from that work. Examples of what mattered to them included doing good work, growing the business, being dependable, reaching their target goals, being a good teammate, creating a healthy, inclusive work environment, looking out for each other, respecting people's lives outside of work. The team acknowledged that all of these values were positive values and worth keeping. They also noticed that some of them conflicted with each other at times, creating stress. They committed to embracing the stress that came with these values and managing them better so they don't become overwhelming. Jessica made notes of the discussion and emailed the team a pdf that graphically depicted the group's list of Worthwhile Stress.

The next week's discussion focused on stress management. For each value identified from the previous week, they discussed as a group what healthy expressions of that value would be and what unhealthy expressions would be. For example, they clarified that "being dependable" in a healthy way would be responding to emails within 24 hours and to not be expected to attend to emails when the office was closed unless it was an urgent matter. An unhealthy expression would be the expectation to immediately respond to emails no matter when they were sent. For each value, everyone had a chance to offer their opinions as to what was healthy and unhealthy, and they reached consensus as a group for each value. Jessica created a blueprint that demonstrated the behavioral boundaries for each of their important values. These boundaries were posted in the conference room and emailed to each staff member. The discussions created a greater level of openness and trust in the group to talk openly about stress and the challenges each staff member faced. It became more evident that this team was comprised of good people doing good work. They just needed to be more communicative about issues that were causing conflict.

The following week's discussion challenged each staff member to express goals associated with each important value and as well as any concerns they were having about expressing those values in daily life. Sheila took this opportunity to express her appreciation that she was a part of a team that valued growing the business and working hard. She noted that and one of her concerns for the business is creating an infrastructure that fostered accessible and inclusive recruitment and retention. Because they were a small company with only one the manager to handle HR issues, she felt that the company took more of a reactive approach to managing personnel issues. "What if we took a more proactive approach to keep the staff we have while recruiting more people with different backgrounds and experience?" She felt like creating a benefits package with more expansive insurance and retirement options would go a long way toward retention and recruitment. She acknowledged that this was a big issue to work through and would require a significant amount of time, but she would be willing to lead a small working group to explore options if a couple of others would be willing to join her and if Jessica would commit to implementing these types of changes. To her surprise, there were two others who said they had the same interest. So that it wouldn't become overwhelming, they decided the working group would spend the next quarter on this project with bi-weekly updates to Jessica and the team. Their goal would be to have a better benefits program in place by the end of the year. The next few meetings comprised of other staff members bringing goals and concerns to the table and developing solutions to address them.

The next phase of meetings involved an open discussion about managing the difficulty of an increasingly relentless world of pace, pressure, and uncertainty. Jessica asked folks to share what their lives looked like outside of work. She emphasized that this wasn't intended to be a complaining session but an honest, open discussion about the real challenges each of them were managing in their lives. She asked them to simply share what was great in their life outside of work, and what was hard. She shared first and because of the previous weeks' discussions, a greater level of trust had been established. Tom shared that he had really appreciated the previous discussions and liked being a part of a team that honored the staff's lives outside of work. He told the team that the greatest, most important part of his life outside of work was his family.

His partner and children were a continually source of support and inspiration. Home was his sanctuary. He wanted to have more qualifications to better support his family which is way it was important to take night courses. The family had been in a stable period for awhile and they had decided this would be a good time to go back to school. While it had made logical sense, he had no idea of how much stress it had added to their lives. He felt overwhelmed and barely treading water at times. He hadn't realized how closed off he had become at work until they started these discussions about stress and wellness. The team responded supportively to Tom's sharing and several opened up about how they had been overwhelmed by commitments they had made outside of work.

Jessica expressed appreciation for their courage in being open about their lives. She knew a colleague who had brought in a psychologist specializing in transitional stress and burnout to do a workshop for their organization. Jessica asked if the team about doing a similar workshop for their company and the team expressed interest in hearing what the psychologist had to say.

The workshop focused on how the brain and body respond to stress and how the mind can exacerbate stress in a manner that starts to eventually strain the body. The psychologist discussed the difference between good stress and distress, and how to start using the mind to manage stress instead of add to it. She mentioned that most people do a pretty good job of finding solutions to problems that are stressful. The stress that is most difficult are the stressors that can't be fixed but are affecting us stressors we have to cope with. The psychologist discussed self-talk that people create which add to stress. She described ten common perfectionistic "shoulds" and expectations people often demand of themselves that only serve to cause undue stress. Tom resonated with the mind trap of needing to reach his potential in all that he does. That was the mantra in his family growing up and he had never questioned it. But now he could see how toxic that self-imposed demand had become.

The psychologist spent the rest of the workshop discussing strategies for effective coping and asked each staff member to write down one strategy from the ones offered that they would commit to trying over the next two months. Then they were asked to share this strategy with the team. Sheila loved the concept of "honoring the reaction, but challenging the conclusion" and wanted to really focus on not catastrophizing when she was feeling strong emotions. Tom shared that he wanted to increase his self-care behaviors and landed on doing some kind of physical exercise twice a week.

The psychologist ended the workshop by taking them through the Wellness Harmony exercise (described in step 4). The team was intrigued by the notion that work-life balance might inhibit flourishing and that a focus on work-life harmony was more effective. He challenged them to share their Harmony Profile results with each other at their next staff meeting. Finally, he congratulated them on creating a cultural norm for taking time each week to discuss wellness and how they were supporting each other through this process. He also reminded them of the additional support that is in the community and the importance of having support in their lives to manage the hardness of this world.

The following weeks included discussions of the Harmony Profile exercise and learning each other's wellness goals for the year. Jessica periodically brought in wellness experts to try out different forms of self-care, such as yoga, mindfulness, creative art, Taiji, small walking groups. Spending 30 minutes a week to openly discuss stress and wellness, the team moved into a space that was more values congruent. They had developed a sense of integrity by challenging themselves AND being healthy in the process. Sheila and her small working group developed a sustainable benefits model that Jessica approved; and Tom got used to applying a more healthy mindset and healthy wellness practices that made his busy life more manageable. While Jessica felt more in charge of the situation than before she also knew that this work was constant and for the organization to continue to flourish the work that the team had been engaged in over the past couple of weeks was only the beginning of creating and maintaining a both/& culture for stressed and well.

References

Crace, R.K., & Crace, R.L. (2020). *Authentic Excellence: Flourishing and resilience in a relentless world.* Routledge.

Crum, A., & Crum, T. (2015). Stress can be a good thing if you know how to use it. *Harvard Business Review.* https://hbr.org/2015/09/stress-can-be-a-good-thing-if-you-know-how-to-use-it

Crum, A.J., Salovey, P., & Achor, S. (2013). Rethinking stress: The role of mindsets in determining the stress response. *Journal of Personality and Social Psychology, 104*(6), 716–733.

Forshaw, M., & Sheffield, D. (Eds.). (2012). *Health psychology in action.* John Wiley & Sons.

Hardy, C.J., & Crace, R.K. (1993). The dimensions of social support when dealing with sport injuries. In D. Pargman (Ed.), *Psychological bases of sport injuries* (pp.121–144). Morgantown, WV: Fitness Information Technology.

Hardy, C.J., Burke, K.L., & Crace, R.K. (2005). Coaching: An effective communication system. In S. Murphy (Ed.), *The sport psych handbook: A complete guide to today's best mental training techniques* (pp.191–212). Champaign, IL: Human Kinetics.

Jamieson, J. P., Nock, M.K., & Mendes, W.B. (2012). Mind over matter: Reappraising arousal improves cardiovascular and cognitive responses to stress. *Journal of Experimental Psychology: General, 141*(3), 417–422. https://doi.org/10.1037/a0025719 (4)

Johnston, D.W. (1993). The current status of the coronary prone behavior pattern. *Journal of the Royal Society of Medicine, 86*(7), 406.

Keller, A., Litzelman, K., Wisk, L.E., Maddox, T., Cheng, E.R., Creswell, P.D., et al. (2012). Does the perception that stress affects health matter? The association with health and mortality. *Health Psychology,* 31(5), 677–684. https://doi.org/10.1037/a0026743 (3).

Lazarus, R.S., & Folkman, S. (1984). *Stress, appraisal, and coping.* Springer Publishing Company. [Google Scholar] (1).

McGonigal, K. (2015). The upside of stress: Why stress is good for you, and how to get good at it. Ny Avery/Penguion Random House. https://www.ted.com/talks/kelly_mcgonigal_how_to_make_stress_your_friend (2)

5

HARD "&" RIGHT

TRANSFORMATIVE OPTIMIZER: VALUES-LED ENGAGEMENT

"Work Through It!" read the sign hanging in Barry's office. The slogan had gotten Barry through a lot: a tough childhood; a career in finance; President of a renowned investment firm; a battle with cancer. However, when faced with a global pandemic and social turmoil, Barry's exhaustive approach led to most of his staff quitting and Barry getting fired.

The Board of Directors conducted a series of interviews with current and former staff members. They wanted to get a better understanding of where Barry's style of leadership went wrong, and to see if there were any promising candidates to replace Barry.

Susan was the first to be interviewed. The Board started with the obvious question: why was she one of the only staff members who hadn't quit?

"Honestly, I don't know why." Susan explained. "Every day I felt like I was at my wits end. Barry piled on so much work when we went remote. He thought we were all slacking because we weren't in the office. But when the schools shutdown, I was basically homeschooling my kids and working a full time job. Then the tragedies on the news; the protests, the election," Susan

DOI: 10.4324/9781003265726-5

was surprised by how much she'd blocked out as she recalled the hardships. "It was all so overwhelming... and important, but honestly, I don't know how I did it... How I'm still doing it." She realized an answer and looked directly at the Board members, "I fought hard to get this job. Working in finance gives my kids stability. I can take care of my mother. And truthfully, I like working with numbers. I like interpreting the fluctuation of business." She leaned back confidently, "I wasn't going to let a workaholic like Barry push me out of a job."

The Board was able to track down Ty who had resigned several months prior. Ty jumped at the chance to relay the problems he was still dealing with after working for Barry, "At first, I was relieved not having to go into the office. Barry was ridiculous. 'Work Through It!' Nothing was ever enough. He couldn't see that he had us working at an unsustainable pace. I kept telling myself, 'Just make it through this project and it'll be easier; Just make it through this week and then you can rest; Just push through today and it'll be ok.'" Ty began to perspire as he recalled, "But Barry just kept giving me more and more work. So, when we went remote, I was thinking I'd be more comfortable in my own space; I could take periodic breaks; Rest here and there without Barry constantly over my shoulder. But it didn't work like that." Ty averted his eyes still feeling affected by the experience. "I started looking at the clock every few minutes, 'Just get through the hour and you can lay down for a minute.' Then I was looking at the clock every minute." Ty looked straight at the board members, "At the end of the day, when I was done working, I couldn't rest. I couldn't exercise. I couldn't read. I couldn't cook. I couldn't call friends. I was worried everything would be too draining for the following workday." Ty calmed himself for a second, "I thought that quitting would be the only way I could find comfort again... but I didn't." Ty confessed, "I immediately started worrying about money and finding a new job, but I'm also scared that I'll wind up working for another Barry. That 'Work Through It!' motto is still haunting me."

Step 1. Recognizing the Or Conflict: When Hard Determines Right or Wrong

There is a relentless uncertainty and stress to our world that creates hardship. Just trying to live a sustainable life can feel overwhelming for individuals. Add to that the complex pressures of a collection of individuals coming together under a common vision, mission, or goal, and you have a perfect storm for "chronic too-muchness." The demands never end, both the proactive demands from strategic plans and the demands that evolve from unforeseen events. Adding the word "too" to anything connotes a negative values judgment. When we feel like we're managing too much, it can create doubt as to whether we can sustain the pace of these pressures. Our life not only becomes characterized by its difficulty but it can restrict our openness to further difficulty. We can start to place a values judgment on hard. Hard can start to feel wrong. Which means that comfort and easy start to feel right. Easy starts to drift into an actual value.

While the desire to move away from hard and toward easy is normal and human, increasing easy to a values level can become disruptive to organizational flourishing. Easy should remain as a preference. Comfort and ease may increase in importance when we are under strain, but they are not values because we get no sense of meaning or purpose from them. So, to artificially elevate them in importance brings an unhealthy competition with true values that have purpose and meaning. A strong tension emerges between a construed value and true values of purpose.

Conversely, to decrease the tension between hard and right, an organization may drift in the opposite direction by dismissing the challenges and hardships of being values-centered. This is what happened in the case with Barry. What had worked for him as a personal motto to manage his life's strife had been generalized to a leadership creed. There was a lack of sensitivity and a muted awareness of strain and its impact on the organization. In these organizations, phrases that speak to self-care or wellness are either absent or felt as hollow and meaningless. The motto becomes "If it's values-centered, then we do it, period, without regard for the toll it takes." But to Barry's employees, the strain of the chronic difficulty started to eclipse the values that drove it. As it became more difficult for employees to draw from values to justify the hard, hard started to feel wrong, relief from hard became the answer, so they left. Even in the case with Ty, the worry of not being financially secure became eclipsed by the sheer burnout of what seemed to feel like "hard for hard's sake," not "hard for right's sake."

Susan made it through, but she made it through by drawing from a deeper level of her personal values. She had accepted the difficulty that felt right for her (advancing professionally, providing for her family) and when things started feeling absurd around her, she relied on those values to sustain her. She accepted a hard that had a personal rightness attached to it, which allowed her to cope with a boss that had lost sight of that. Whether it's chasing comfort or chasing values without regard for hard, it's clear that this "Or" tension compromises organizational flourishing.

Step 2. Finding the Purpose of &: Values-Led Engagement

How do we create capacity for both/& – carrying hard & right? We all have a relationship with fear, comfort, and our values. All three are interdependent. We can't fear anything that is unimportant; and if we live by our values, which can be challenging and hard, we must have some restorative time. What is critical for flourishing is determining which relationship leads most of the time. While we are naturally motivated by fear and comfort, the deepest motivator is our values. It is a motivation that can override fear and fatigue, when properly managed. But it requires thinking differently about values. It requires a paradigm shift of moving from values clarification to values relationship; from what our values are to how our values are alive in our lives. When we are aware of how values are active in our lives, we are more aware of what is truly guiding our behavior – purpose or fear-based reactivity.

It is easy to take a passive approach to our values. That can mean we either don't tune in frequently enough to assess what is important to us, or we believe that just clarifying what matters is sufficient. As with all relationships, developing a healthy relationship with values requires time and effort. But a passive approach to values results in fear and/or comfort leading most of the time resulting in us "living by our neurology." Our bodies are neurologically wired for crisis and regulation. So, it's easy to settle into a rhythm of daily living that is about attending to all of the critical "have to's" of the day and then seeking comfort. There is nothing wrong with that per se, it's how we're naturally wired to behave. But imagine all individuals in an organization behaving in that manner. What happens to values? Mission statements, organizational vision, and values start to become platitudes that are hung on the walls but can become distant in our awareness and behavior. While we are neurologically primed for this type of living, it's not congruent with who we are as a species. Humans are a purposeful and relational species. In order to flourish, we must move beyond our neurology and be more attentive to living with purpose. But that's not enough, we must tune into how our lived purpose impacts others and how others' lived purpose impacts us. And with the tension between hard and right, if we're not in a closer, healthier relationship with our values, we will gravitate toward managing hard by seeking comfort.

Comfort can take the form of moving toward easy, or it can take the form of moving toward the familiar or what is habitual. In Barry's case, he had managed fear and adversity by working hard, period. During the pandemic and social crises, he mistakenly assumed his approach was the best approach for the whole organization. Rather than proceeding with what was more familiar to him, he could have spent time assessing the team to learn that a small adaptation to his approach would have made a big difference. If Barry could have found a way to consistently message, "Courageously work through what's right, and support each other along the way," It would have acknowledged why "working through it" was important. That it's hard and courageous work, and we can only work through it if we support each other through the difficulty. That is the essence of authentic excellence in organizations – adopting the ability to carry hard **and** right rather than focusing on hard **or** right.

Organizations shift their motivation from being fear-based to values-led when they fully identify prominent values; clarify how those values look in action; understand the challenges and opportunities those values bring to their organization; and develop ways to manage those values in a healthy manner (Lencioni, 2020; Kotter, 2012; Sinek, 2009). This shift transforms the meaning of "hard" to being perceived as an acceptable reality of values-led behavior amidst uncertainty, rather than a problem that needs to be fixed. Easy fades from being a value to being something that can be appreciated when it's there but not a goal for which to strive.

When the transformative optimizer, Values-Led Engagement, exists, there is also a shift in how motivation is perceived. It's a shift from trying to *be* motivated to *understanding* motivation and focusing more on engagement rather than willpower. Motivation is a function of our thoughts, emotions, energies, and abilities. When those are all flowing in the same direction, motivation just happens. When we have to think about motivating ourselves, it means one or more of those factors are flowing upstream. Seeking to more deeply understand how those factors are playing out helps us manage motivation better at both individual and organizational levels.

Relying on willpower is an ineffective strategy because it ironically causes us to be overly emotion-centered. The typical scenario for an organization (as well as individuals) is that there is a clarification of what is important. From that clarification, there is an expectation that motivation and action will naturally flow from that clarification. However, as we have learned, clarifying one's values actually causes ambivalence due to the uncertainty and potential cost of failing at the things that are important. The demand for willpower sets us up to expect a surge of motivation when we start to engage in our purposeful goals. When we experience ambivalence instead, we worry about what's wrong with us and judge ourselves as insufficiently self-disciplined or motivated. When we flourish, we embrace both the purpose AND the challenge. We acknowledge the uncertainty, embrace the ambivalence and the difficulty, and engage in the purpose. This requires intentional and consistent work to develop that level of relationship and engagement with our values. What does that work look like?

Step 3. Analyzing Your Team – Clarifying the "Worthy Difficulties"

To be clear, not all purposeful behavior has to be hard. Organizations can develop rhythms to values-centered behavior that can be enjoyable and comfortable. Those should be mindfully appreciated and celebrated, but not become the standard for which to strive. In the same vein, not all hard behavior should be ascribed "right" just because it's hard. It takes time and discernment for an organization to clarify what "hards" are worthy and warrant engagement.

Clarifying Worthy "Hards"

- What are the prominent team values? Using the Group Feature of the LVI Online, assess the prominent group values as described in Chapter 2, Personal Values & Common Values. Spend time exploring as a group the prominent values of the team.
- What is the purpose and meaning behind each of these values at this point in time in the organization?
- How do those prominent team values look in action?
- What is hard and what is easy about those values in action?
- What do these values look like in action when they are healthy and when they are unhealthy?

Understanding Motivation and Decision-Making in Your Organization

- How is motivation discussed in your organization?
- What organizational practices are explicitly intended to motivate?
- What underlying norms or communications exist that hold more motivational power than explicit practices and policies?
- What practices exist that unintentionally undermine motivation?
- What does the process of decision-making look like in your organization? How are things decided and communicated once a decision has been made?

The Board appointed Susan as the interim manager to replace Barry. Her first order of business was to call the team together for a half day retreat. She didn't want the focus to be solely about the problems of the past but wanted everyone to have a voice as they moved forward. She facilitated a discussion based on questions (listed above) designed to re-engage the values and behaviors that felt worthy of the team's efforts.

From the retreat, Susan learned a lot, but there were a few immediate takeaways that were important to address. It wasn't surprising that Responsibility and Achievement were their Top Team values. She could see that Barry had called upon those values but in a manner that was unhealthy. A key insight for Susan was that she had not considered values as having the potential of being unhealthy. She had just assumed that values were always positive, but the past few months were clear evidence of how values could go awry. As Susan and the team discussed a healthy expression of Responsibility for the first time, they redefined the value in action as being dependable to each other with goals that were collectively agreed upon. The team also redefined Achievement as valuing hard work and to include in that hard work the challenge of seeing wellness as essential to excellence. She was also surprised to see how Interdependence and Creativity were prominent values. The importance of "team" mattered more to this group than she had expected. And Creativity wasn't even discussed under Barry's leadership, yet it was a high priority value for most of the team.

This initial discussion of values and decision-making helped Susan understand that most major decisions were made through Barry's personal values lens and decision-making style. Barry was very independent-minded and believed that with his leadership position came the responsibility of making decisions. This combination led to decisions being made without much engagement or consultation of the team. Through the values discussion, Susan could see how and why Barry led the way he did. He felt it was his responsibility to be the decision-maker. When the pandemic hit, the overwhelming uncertainty created an atmosphere of fear that shifted Barry's values of Independence and Responsibility into a hyper-drive need for control. The retreat allowed Susan to gain a deeper understanding of how Barry drifted into his pattern of behavior.

She started to get a better feel for what was truly important to the team and understand the process of how they made decisions —what their "worthy difficulties" were.

Step 4. Readying for &: Game Plan for Values-Led Engagement

Worthy Difficulties in Action

After a group works through the initial values-based analysis questions from Step 3, it is important to dive deeper into what those values look like in action and as healthy expressions. All voices matter during this stage of planning.

As in the group values exercise from Chapter 2, review the organization's collective High Priority values and have a discussion about what each value means to the organization using the team's normative language. It's appropriate to align the name and meaning of a value to be more congruent with the team. With each value, discuss both the positive nature of the value and the challenges associated with the value. Discuss what these values look like in action (i.e., if people could only observe the team's behavior, how would they know that this is a team value?). What does each value look like when it's healthy and when it's unhealthy? What contributes to it being healthy and unhealthy?

Discuss the Over-Attention values. These are values where worries, fears, and needs have driven the group to give more attention to them than they prefer. What would these values look like in action if they were more healthfully expressed? Can any of the fears and worries that drive these values into Over-Attention be challenged and addressed directly?

Discuss the Under-Attention values and decide collectively on one or two Under-Attention values to devote more time to and what that would look like?

Discuss the Medium/Low Priority values and examine how team members who hold some of those values as high may at times feel marginalized. Discuss, as a team, ways to honor diverse values and perspectives even if they are only periodically or seldom expressed as an organization. Encourage the norm of active curiosity to build an appreciation, understanding, and empathy for diverse values. Remind the team that a strong predictor of organizational flourishing is diversity of values and perspectives.

From this extensive discussion, clarify the "Worthy Difficulties," the goals and actions in the organization that align with a healthy expression of values. Brainstorm ways to periodically honor and celebrate both the team's engagement in Worthy Difficulties, as well as the experiences that have been unexpectedly easy.

Confident Values-Led Decision-Making (Force Field Analysis)

Organizations can more consistently experience values-led engagement if they are more intentional about incorporating values into their decision-making process. This is especially important when organizations are trying to choose between two "rights." Rather than use traditional balance sheet approaches or pro/con lists, a values-centered adaptation of Force Field Analysis may be helpful.

The process involves clarifying the issue for which a decision needs to be made and initially choosing one side of that equation. For instance, a group may be trying to decide whether to work remotely half of the week or work in the office full time, and they decide to analyze the decision on the premise that they will work remotely half of the week. From that premise, brainstorm a list of all the facilitative forces or factors that would move the group toward working remotely. Then brainstorm a list of restrictive forces or factors that would move the group away from that decision. Once the complete lists of facilitative and restraining factors are clarified, return to each item on both lists and rate each item from 1–10 how important that item is to the organization at this point in time with 10 being very important and 1 being very unimportant. Then rate each item on both lists as to how realistic or probable that item is with 10 being very probable and 1 being very improbable. For instance, one factor may be "If we don't allow for remote work, we won't be able to successfully recruit new employees. We'll become stagnant and be out of business in three years." It's important to clarify how realistic or probable that factor is. From this analysis, patterns will often emerge as the factors that are most values congruent have the most salience; conversely fears and worries may expose patterns that cause possible factors to feel like probable factors.

Step 5. Giving Voice to &: From Game Plan to Action

Several months later, Susan's organization continued discussions on team values in a weekend retreat off-site. They transitioned from analyzing what their team values were to a lengthier discussion about what they looked like in action, how they were positive and effective, and under what circumstances did they become unhealthy. Their top five team values were Responsibility, Achievement, Interdependence, Creativity, and Objective Analysis. The team personalized these values to mean being dependable to each other and their customers, working hard grow the company, being team-oriented, and continuing to think creatively and analytically about their work.

Their Over-Attention values were Responsibility and Achievement. Half of the team put these values in High Priority and half of them put them in Over-Attention. It was clear that these values were important to everyone but many had felt the team had lost perspective on these values — that Responsibility and Achievement had drifted into needs or virtues that were sacred and couldn't be challenged. They felt that the concept of stress glorification could be applied to how some in the organization regarded Achievement where everyone seemed to be continually trying to one-up each other as to how hard they were working.

The team went on to define healthy expression for Responsibility as "trusting each other to do their jobs and seeing Responsibility to the team and responsibility to life outside of work as mutually important." Unhealthy expression of Responsibility was defined as "work through it." Healthy expression of Achievement became "working hard on agreed-upon goals and acknowledging that all their goals could rarely be accomplished in a day." The team's unhealthy expression of Achievement utilized the principle of maximal work instead of optimal work where achievement was chronically defined by outcomes rather than engagement.

The most notable Under-Attention value was Health & Activity. They decided to integrate Health & Activity into their values of Responsibility, Achievement, and Interdependence. Wellness would now be considered an expression of all three of these values. Susan also had the opportunity to talk about how she felt her values of Concern for the Environment and Spirituality were values she couldn't talk about at work which was confirmed by the team aggregate placing those values in the Low Priority category. While she didn't expect those to be high values of the organization, it felt better to have space to talk about why those values were important to her and how she expresses them outside of work.

The team came to a consensus about motivation. When fear was the primary motivation, this resulted in unhealthy expressions of values that led to burnout and loss of morale. When there was a healthy engagement in their values, they noticed that motivation wasn't even a point of focus. They began to understand the deeper levels of motivation generated by healthy expression of values.

Near the end of the retreat, they brainstormed how they could integrate the concepts of stress celebration and stress support into their company traditions. On a monthly basis, they would honor and celebrate the meaning and fulfillment they got from their hard work. The celebrations would be in the form of enjoyable wellness activities, such as a catered meal after the end of a project or an outing at a local river cruise. They also developed stress support partners who would support and encourage each other through their hard work.

At the next staff meeting, they used the Force Field Analysis process to tackle an issue that had been a source of anxiety for awhile. Before the pandemic, they had planned to expand their office space and add a new Emerging Technologies department with additional staff. During the pandemic, that topic was shelved and the focus became company survival. Despite the fear and anxiety, the company had not suffered as much as they had predicted. If anything threatened the company, it was the unsustainable climate that Barry had created. When they returned to the topic of "how do we want to grow and develop as a company," the opportunity to expand into a new arena was exciting . . . and scary. By going through the analysis, they clarified that the timing was probably another year away but that this issue was important enough to spend time planning and preparing for expansion over this next year. The team believed most of the reasons for not expanding were fear-based which had not been clear when considering expansion during the pandemic. At the end of that meeting, Susan found herself unexpectedly needing to do her own personal Force Field Analysis because she was offered the lead manager position. If she decided to accept the position, she knew her first action would be to call Ty and encourage him to return.

References

Lencioni, P. (2020). *The motive: Why so many leaders abdicate their most important responsibilities.* Wiley.

Kotter, J.P. (2012). *Leading change.* Harvard Business Review Press.

Sinek, S. (2009). *Start with why: How great leaders inspire everyone to take action.* Portfolio/Penguion.

6

INNOVATION "&" TRADITION

TRANSFORMATIVE OPTIMIZER:
OPTIMAL CHANGE ADAPTABILITY

The Water Quality Division of Ohio's State Department had always been minimally funded. The division's annual budget had been marginal for the past 15 years. Julia, Ron, Aisha, and Max made up the division's entire staff. All four had worked together at the division for over ten years. The budget, the staff, the day-to-day operations, the expectations had remained the same for so long that the four staff members ran the division quite efficiently. They all had a clear understanding of what could be adequately accomplished with their budget constraints and what projects were not feasible. Things ran smoothly until two years ago when The Water Quality Division received nearly ten times their annual budget.

A powerful politician ran on a platform that promised to update and organize the state's environmental municipal systems. When the politician won the election, funding was immediately allotted to divisions like Water Quality. Seemingly overnight, Julia, Ron, Aisha, and Max were inundated with new projects, procedures, and expectations.

The first step was to hire more staff. The four employees had worked together for so long that they inherently knew each other's strengths and

DOI: 10.4324/9781003265726-6

how to share specific jobs for each project. As they started to interview candidates, they realized that any new hire would reset most work dynamics that had become automatic.

It started with four new hires. The new employees had different education backgrounds and work experiences, but they shared a common concern for the outdated state of the division's systems.

"I should start digitizing these records." Nica, one of the new hires, suggested. "These go back almost 20 years. Have any digitized records been established?" Nica asked Ron.

"We don't do that here." Ron replied finding an excuse to walk away.

Of the four original employees, Aisha was most willing to adapt to changes even when she still felt lost. "I don't know how to use CAD." She explained to one of the new employees asking for help on a treatment center design project. "Can you show me the basics?"

Julia, who like Ron had resisted the changes, was afraid to admit that she hadn't used any Computer Aided Design programs before. She had been named project manager for the treatment center, and at first assigned work to new hires but when a new employee asked, "What CAD program do you use here?" Julia reassigned the work to Ron and Max.

While the legacy staff hoarded projects, the new hires became proactive in their endeavors. The projects they did work on were getting noticed by other municipal divisions as innovative and cost-effective. They were finding sustainable, natural ways to protect and treat municipal water. Eventually, the newer hires became recognized by other departments and politicians as figureheads of the Water Quality Division. A power shift began to develop were the new staff who hired even newer staff were managing and delegating the projects.

Aisha, Max, Ron, and Julia were initially receptive to the shift in management. As long as they did an average job with the work they were assigned, their jobs weren't in danger. In fact, they enjoyed not having to deal with the decision-making pressures that came with being project manager. They even improved their skills working with newer functions like CAD, digitizing records, and creative environmental solutions. Despite growth in the division, a new exhaustion began to develop.

There was an enthusiasm among the growing staff at The Water Quality Division. An adequately funded environmental division provided a rare opportunity for employees to invent, attempt, and enact strategies they could only case study at school or pitch to reluctant organizations. But while *the enthusiasm and new energy produced innovative treatment plans, the division was getting bogged down and fatigued by their approach to these projects. The newer management staff seemed to be reinventing the wheel with each new project. They shuffled staff members who worked well together so that teams with complementary strengths were regularly broken up and rearranged. Any team traction or cohesion that had materialized in previous projects was being disregarded because the enthusiasm for trying out new ideas and strategies dominated office function.*

Step 1. Recognizing the Or Conflict: Change – A Catalyst for Fear, Loss, and Excitement

The inevitability of change, or the certainty of uncertainty, is a universal human experience. We are dynamic creatures living in a dynamic world. Despite its inevitability, change remains an uncomfortable experience for many because of the associated ambiguity and ambivalence. With change we are always leaving something and what we're heading to is uncertain. Our brain processes that as loss and fear. For some, the perceived loss is felt as minor and for others, it's a full grieving process. For some, the uncertainty is exciting and for others, it's anxiety-provoking. With such wide ranges of emotions and thoughts, we can easily adopt a protective position. Fear can cause us to protect ourselves from potential hurt by avoiding change until it's absolutely necessary or by being over-controlling and perfectionistic. Paradoxically, as individuals, our natural protective attempts to be protective end up causing more stress in the long run. The stress of stepping into something at the last minute due to avoidance, or the stress of chronic worry due to trying to control everything eventually creates strain that's unsustainable. Now imagine how individual responses ranging between avoidance and perfectionism can coalesce in an organization.

At an organizational level, change is simply disruptive. Change can disrupt rhythm, tradition, habit, and security. How many times have you heard in your organization, "This has been a tough year due to unexpected changes, but next year will be better, we'll find our stride again," only to find the same statement occurring year after year due to other changes? Just the thought, "next year will be better," reveals how disruptive change can feel and how badly we can want things to stabilize. Change can be a catalyst for fear, loss, excitement, and disruption, so it requires careful attention (Kotter, 2014; Kotter & Cohen, 2002; Kotter, Akhtar, & Gupta, 2021).

If we don't develop healthy ways of managing our responses to change, organizations tend to settle into one side of the equation to ease the tension. Organizations can create ritualistic traditions to resist change and frame the status quo as "stability." "We don't do that here" can be a commonly used phrase. Resistance to change can be done through avoidance or over-control. Organizations can avoid the obvious signs of change around them, having a myopic vision that only looks for reasons to stay the same. Or they can use power and platitudes to control policies and procedures that enable rigid adherence to sameness. The impact of resistance to change can be stagnation in the midst of a constantly evolving society.

Conversely, an organization that prizes change can, at times, invoke change just for change's sake, framing it as progressive innovation. The impact of constant change makes it challenging for longitudinal assessment, continuity of operations across cohorts, and pressure to constantly innovate. Celebrating change can be perpetuated through avoidance and over-control. Avoidance can take the form of not putting any energy or resources toward traditions, while over-control can highly reward those staff who are the most creative and innovative – devaluing actions that perpetuate the status quo.

Both extremes can create a rigidity that negatively impacts the developmental growth of an organization. It can also pendulum swing during cohort transitions. Take the Water Quality example. It shows how change can be stressful during the best of times, such as a long-term commitment to substantial resources. The first generation of employees found comfort in stability while the second generation reveled in constant change. People gravitated toward their comfort zone as it pertained to change. Some avoided and blended into the woodwork; others took control with intensity. Both proved to be less effective. The degree to which organizations manage both values and fear determines whether change is highly or minimally disruptive.

Step 2. Finding the Purpose of &: Remove the Blinders, Keep the Shades

What occurs when change and tradition coexist healthfully? Imagine an openness to change that still has boundaries and limits. Imagine traditions and company mottos that honor legacy while being open to redefinition with every new cohort or important transition. Imagine a team culture that embraces an industry's rhythm of change, that understands a company's historical response to change, and that understands the individual variability of how change is perceived. When change and tradition authentically coexist, optimal adaptability to change can occur. There is an agility and courage to adapting to change. It requires a sensitivity, attention, and analysis of several key variables: (1) fear management; (2) adult development; (3) whether a transition is reactive or proactive; (4) an openness to learning from the impact of past changes and transitions; (5) an industry's rhythm and historical track record of change; and (6) understanding the distinction between tradition, ritual, and routine. Perceptual blinders about change are removed but boundaries retain function so that change doesn't go unbridled.

Uncertainty about things we deem important evokes fear in our brain, which we naturally respond to with control or avoidance. We either jump in with both feet; wait and see how things evolve before committing; or we hide until it's safe. Fear creates behavioral and perceptual blinders. Julia was an example of the avoidance response, and as they gained power, the new staff exhibited the more controlling response. We see what we want to see and we justify our behavior through narratives that enable the behavior to continue. And there is just enough ambiguity with change to justify our reasoning. "No risk it, no biscuit." "No guts, no glory." "Look before you leap." "Don't write checks you can't cash." Take your pick. What does the saying you're most drawn to reveal about your feelings of change?

How we respond to ambiguity, though, is not just a function of fear. There's a *developmental process* to sitting with the ambiguity of change. One of the most crucial developmental tasks of being an adult is developing a tolerance for ambiguity. As adolescents and emerging adults, we generally have less tolerance for ambiguity. At that stage, we see the world through a dichotomized, all-or-nothing, black or white lens. The dichotomized lens is present in young stages of moral development, identity development, self-perception, and view of the world. As people start learning about the ambiguities of the world in emerging adulthood, there is a dissonance. At first, we will try to fit a grey world into a black & white model. But it can't be sustained. Over time, maturity and living through various personal ambiguities start to grow into a tolerance for ambiguity, and therefore, a greater adaptability to change. More importantly, innovation is developmentally forward moving and progressive. So, when tradition and innovation coexist, the creative aspect of innovation provides a developmental spark that can move both individuals and organizations to a higher tolerance and embracing of ambiguity.

But this is why healthy *fear management* is so important. Typically, adults grow into an adaptability to change, but only if they develop healthy ways of managing fear. If they get locked into a controlling/avoidance paradigm of fear management and are enabled to continue that approach, it becomes developmentally arresting to where they stay stuck until the environment forces them into growing through it. You can even see older adults in organizations with enough privilege and power to continue responding to change in this manner.

Whether a transition is *reactive or proactive* can influence how an organization responds. One is not better than the other, the pressure points and types of reactions just tend to be different. *Reactive or unplanned transitions* are changes that organizations didn't anticipate but find themselves managing. Examples are the unexpected departure of an employee, the death or illness of an employee, or an unexpected social or economic issue that significantly impacts the organization. The Water Quality Division had operated under the same economic parameters for decades and then suddenly the political climate changed and they found themselves with resources they had not anticipated. During a reactive transition, there is rarely a neutral response by individuals whose reactions can be mixed with grief and fear. Time needs to be given to these reactions before major decisions and policies are made. With *proactive transitions*, change is on the horizon that an organization can see and plan for. Examples include upcoming shifts in generational cohorts like retirement, anticipated changes in industry, anticipated changes in leadership, or anticipated changes in social or political climates that will impact the organization. Intuitively, it would seem that this would be an easier transition because it's known. On the contrary, anticipatory anxiety can often be more disruptive. Such anxiety can create multiple "what if" scenarios that are fear driven. Decisions can be made based on avoidance of the "what ifs," rather than an organization's values. Anticipatory grief may also play a part where individuals start reacting to the upcoming change before it occurs. Anticipatory anxiety and anticipatory grief tend to create a pressure that is much worse than the eventual reality, but it can significantly impact how well a company manages change, and again, much of it comes down to healthy fear management.

Organizations that are excited by change for change's sake don't benefit from valuable lessons that are available from the past. By allowing both innovation and tradition to exist, the past still has value, which means that the past is open for reflection and analysis. What has been the *history of an organization's response to change?* Looking back with 20/20 hindsight and the full knowledge of impact, what were the true reasons behind the organization's response to change? What themes emerge? What blind spots or sensitivities emerge? What was the impact of the responses to change over time? When did the response work out well? When did they not? Diving into such questions provides the benefit and brilliance of optimal change adaptability. It allows for the past to create innovation, to step into change positively having learned and grown from the past.

Optimal change adaptability also includes *awareness of the overall industry* – a sensitivity to the rhythm of change that exists at a macro level beyond the organization to include the entire industry. Is there a natural, longitudinal rhythm to change that is predictable? How is an industry typically impacted by socio-cultural issues? What has been the industry's response to past change that has turned out effective and ineffective? Allowing tradition and innovation to coexist creates an analytical approach at a broader systems level and allows for a think-tank approach to solving problems that seem more industry-laden than organization specific.

To fully embrace the coexistence of tradition and innovation, an organization needs to clarify between *rituals, traditions, and routine.* Organizations often equate rituals and traditions. They are not the same. In the same way that rituals are not the same as routines. The most important takeaway is that *Rituals control you, while you control routines and traditions.* Rituals are developed as a way to create a sense of control among the uncertainty of life. The organizations with the least amount of control in their outcomes tend to have the highest superstitions and rituals as a way of "feeling" in control. Take the sport of baseball. A highly successful performance in baseball equates to failing twice as much as you succeed (i.e., a.333 batting average). Baseball teams tend to develop many rituals and superstitions to maintain a sense of confidence in control. Organizations can create rituals that are intended to promote a sense of connection, loyalty, focus, and performance. But rituals can become rigid and sacred to the point where they can't be challenged or revisited. To challenge rituals is to be disloyal to the organization.

Routines and traditions differ from rituals. They are not about control but about optimizing effectiveness and creating a flexible connection between cohorts and generations. Routines are processes that promote an effective mindset. For instance, a person may know that they work better when they get up at a certain time, exercise, have a good breakfast, and do a brief meditation before they start their work. They've learned these steps facilitate a proper mindset for effectiveness. Organizations can develop similar routines that optimize focus, engagement, and importance. They may schedule meetings and retreats at particular times they've learned to be optimal for subsequent work. However, care needs to be taken that routines don't drift into being rituals. We have seen companies develop routines that at first were optimizing but eventually became so dogmatic that if the routine wasn't followed, then there was the belief that it was going to be a bad day. For instance, a company implements a brief morning meditation at the beginning of each day, and at first, there is a noticeable difference in how people enter the challenges of their day with acceptance and focus. However, it quickly becomes a ritual to where those that don't attend are negatively judged and on days when the meditation does not occur, there is a conclusion that the day is going to be unproductive.

While routines are regular processes that facilitate present, organizational goals; traditions are a way to bridge a sense of longitudinal connection to past, present, and future. Traditions are experiences and processes that serve to remind people of the deeper values and mission of an organization. But traditions are flexible and adaptable to cohorts across time. Take, for example, a company who has used the motto "Team Unity" for several generations. In the first generation, Team Unity was defined as everyone thinking and valuing the same as the company leader. The expectation was to attend every holiday gathering and every quarterly retreat to hear the charismatic words and philosophy of the company leader. If this were a ritual, then there could be no departure from full engagement at these events without severe judgment. However, as a tradition, flexibility was built into the term "unity." Each year, they would come together as a company and decide what Team Unity meant. Some concepts and procedures were enduring over the years, but some processes changed as a function of new people entering the company culture. Diversity of experiences brought new meaning to the term "unity." New experiences, new events, and new processes still connected to tradition were established. What remained constant was the importance of unity and doing something regularly that connected the mindset deeper into purpose beyond the day-to-day operations.

Step 3. Analyzing Your Team – How Does Change Land Here?

Answer the following questions to gauge how adaptable your organization is to change:

1. What's your first reaction when the possibility of change is brought to your awareness? Where would you put yourself on the continuum between resistance and excitement? From your initial reaction to the possibility of change, how long does it usually take you to land in a place that feels healthy and confident for you? How do those close to you initially react to change? How does their reaction impact you emotionally and psychologically?

2. How does your organizational culture first react to the possibility of change? How does the organization's reaction impact you? How long does it take your organization to land in a place that feels healthy and rhythmic?

3. What is your organization's typical response to issues that trigger fear and anxiety? Is over-control or avoidance a pattern in your organization around these issues? How does your organization manage ambiguity and ambivalence?

4. Thinking over time, what is your organization's past track record of managing change? What were key factors influencing how your organization managed change? Looking back with 20/20 hindsight and the full knowledge of impact, are there more reasons behind the organization's response to change? What themes emerge?

5. Is your organization currently managing a reactive or proactive transition? What have been the reactions to this transition thus far?

6. At a macro, industry level, is there a natural, longitudinal rhythm to change that is predictable? How is your industry affected by socio-cultural issues? What have been effective and ineffective industry responses to past change?

7. Does your organization have traditions, rituals, or routines? How often are they revisited or revised to maintain relevance?

Step 4. Readying for &: Holding Fear Well – The Key to Optimal Change Adaptability

In Step 2, we discussed several factors that influence how well an organization adapts to change and embraces both tradition and innovation. Fortunately, most of these factors can be addressed and understood by openly discussing them as a group. The one factor that most stands in the way is fear management. Managing the uncertainty of change or the fear of moving from tradition is a challenge. But unless that challenge is taken on, an organization is vulnerable to rigidly adhering to obsolete tradition out of fear, resulting in effective rituals. They are vulnerable to resisting change and not learning from their history, resulting in poor adaptation to transition. Conversely, managing fear of stagnation and routine can result inefficient changing for change's sake.

Stepping into the challenge of fear management is a crucial step toward optimal change adaptability. One of the difficulties of fear management is that it is an individual endeavor. This is one of those organizational tasks that is individually focused. So, the organization's role is to affirm, advocate, and support the importance of this work for each individual. Organizational support makes a significant difference with individual commitment to the difficult task of fear management.

Six Strategies for Holding Fear Well

There is a dynamic relationship between values and fear. When you dare to care about something, stakes become involved. Many of us are taught how to care, but not how to manage the fear associated with caring. Fear-based excellence brings fear to the foreground to kick-start the nervous system into action through over-control or avoidance. Does that mean when people flourish they are less afraid? No, they hold fear well. People who manage fear well understand that because of uncertainty fear will always accompany what is important to them. The objective is to keep fear in perspective so that values stay in the foreground. We discuss six strategies for managing fear of failure optimally (Crace & Crace, 2020). The goal of each of these strategies is to move fear into its sweet spot, where it keeps us alert but is not our primary driver.

Strategy #1: Moving from Perceiving Fear as an Emotion of Threat, to an Emotion of Importance

Fear is an uncomfortable emotion, both physically and mentally. The unpleasant "what if" scenarios we can formulate in our mind make it very easy to see fear as an emotion of threat. One of the distinctions we found when analyzing people who consistently flourish is that they intentionally process the emotion of fear differently. They see it as an emotion associated with importance confirming that they are engaged in meaningful behavior. They get worried if they are not feeling the pressure associated with fear of failure. When we flourish, we accept and embrace fear as a necessary companion to living a values-based life. The mindset is learning to view evidence of fear as a good sign of engagement in something that is personally right. Learning to embrace the feeling of fear while courageously stepping into a path that is right is more effective than waiting to be unafraid. In early studies that examined bystander behavior, fear was a common reason why people didn't help others. Consequently, many of the bystander training models focused on fear reduction strategies. Unfortunately, fear reduction training has not been shown to be highly effective in influencing bystander behavior. Part of the reason is that when people commit courageous acts, they are not unafraid; something just becomes more important than their fear. Seeing fear as an emotion associated with personal importance can shift us from the need to distance ourselves from fear.

Strategy #2: Moving from Perceiving Failure as a Personal Statement, to an Experience of Worthy Disappointment

The fear of not attaining the outcomes we work so hard for can become very personal. When we experience "failure" it's very easy to attach future implications to that failure experience. "What does this month of bad performance mean for my future ability to advance in this organization?" "What does this challenging time with my supervisor mean for job security here?" It's normal to place future meaning on present outcomes. But when we personalize failure, it sharply amplifies our fear. To keep fear in its proper perspective, it is important to see unattained outcomes as worthy disappointments. When people flourish they honor the sting of disappointing outcomes, and they don't see it as anything more than that. They try to learn from disappointing outcomes without concluding personal or future implications. To see something as a personal failure is overwhelming and brings the fear of experiencing failure to the foreground. Perceiving failure as a worthy disappointment can help because humans tend to be more confident in their ability to manage and process disappointment. People feel less confident in processing failure and personal conclusions which often times require special coping strategies.

Strategy #3: Moving from Perceiving Hurt as Awful (Requiring Protection) to Viewing Hurt as a Difficult Emotion (And Only Difficult)

No one likes to feel hurt, but when we see hurt as an awful thing, we become preoccupied with avoiding it at all costs. This sends fear to the foreground. To flourish, we must deconstruct hurt and see it for what it truly is, a difficult emotion. If we accept hurt as hard, and nothing more than hard, we become less afraid of it. We never like hurt, but if we categorize it as hard and not awful, then it doesn't get in our way as much. Values can lead when the only risk is processing something difficult. The fear associated with organizational change is often due to "what if" thinking that creates a possible scenario that results in possible hurt, resulting in resistance. Recognizing that fear causes us to perceive a possibility as probable, and looking more at the probable opportunities that change provides can help a person hold the uncertainty in a healthy manner.

Many people, especially those in marginalized communities, experience reoccurring hurt stemming from systemic prejudice. This strategy is not meant to diminish the validity of that hurt nor to undermine the difficulty of processing that hurt. The point of this strategy is to break up the pain of chronic hurt into temporary periods of varying intensity. In doing so, the goal is to help prevent one's life from being obstructed by chronic protection from hurt.

Strategy #4: Shifting from Experiential Confidence to Volitional Confidence

There are two kinds of confidence. The one we are most familiar with is experiential confidence, "The more experience I have the more confidence I feel." Experiential confidence can also be defined as, "I feel more confident when I am having a better experience." When we do well early on in a performance, we can ride a wave of confidence. Also, if we're in the middle of a difficult performance and something happens that shifts the momentum (e.g., positive crowd response) in our favor, we use that shift to gain confidence. But if that momentum shift doesn't happen, we can prematurely conclude that this wasn't our day and submit to our fears and frustrations. Experiential confidence is limited by factors we cannot control. The more our confidence is reliant on those uncertain factors, the more insecure we are, and the more we will turn to over-control and avoidance as a way of coping. Basing our confidence on the amount we have prepared or experienced is a form of over-control. When we only rely on experiential confidence, fear becomes overwhelming in unexpected or uncertain scenarios like Jay's example. That is why performers will often use superstitious rituals to feel more in control.

While experiential confidence isn't a bad thing, it is limited. There is another type of confidence that can be utilized to avoid the pitfalls of experiential confidence, volitional confidence. Volitional confidence is confidence by choice. It essentially means, "When I feel that I can't, what of this CAN I do?" Volitional confidence can help counteract fear-based coping patterns. Focusing on, "What of this can I do," bypasses reliance on preparation. For someone, who copes with fear through over-control and over-preparation, choosing to work with what you have in situations where you are unable to prepare can move one beyond their neurological patterns to a place of flow. Additionally, for those who are prone to coping with fear through avoidance and procrastination, focusing on, "What of this can I do," breaks the task down to approachable portions. There are many situations when we intend to spend time on an important project but find ourselves avoiding that work out of fear or discomfort. When the time comes to do the work, we begin thinking of ways to avoid having to step into that hard work. At that moment when we feel the pull of "can't," we can say, "What of this CAN I do at this time?" Even if the answer is, "I can work on this for ten minutes," it moves one beyond their neurological patterns to a place of productivity. Whenever our behavior follows "can't," we give more power to the motivational pull of fear and comfort. Whenever we step into "can," no matter how small a step it is, we lead with values and it starts to change how we process fear (Greenberg, 2017; Schwartz, 2011; Schwartz & Begley, 2002; Schwartz & Beyette, 1997; Schwartz, Stapp & Beauregard, 2004).

Strategy #5: Moving from Striving for Passion, Happiness, Potential, and Balance to Striving for Purpose, Meaning, Expression, and Harmony

How many times have you heard the importance of pursuing your passion, striving to do what makes you happy, reaching for your potential, or balancing life and work? They are wonderful concepts. They also get in our way because they pull fear to the foreground. Living with passion and happiness causes us to become highly sensitive to how we're feeling. But emotions can be affected by many factors beyond our control. If we're constantly striving for passion and happiness, what happens if we go through a couple of weeks of not feeling either? Two responses tend to happen that work against us. First, we can become very evaluative and start questioning whether we're doing the right thing. Second, we can put pressure on ourselves to search for something that will help us feel better as soon as possible which may or may not be healthy or congruent with our values.

The same problem occurs with the concepts of striving for our potential and work/life balance. Striving for potential is supposed to motivate us. Striving for work/life balance is supposed to keep us healthy. Neither is very effective in accomplishing those goals. Potential is actually a false concept founded in fear and mistrust. While it's a wonderful cliché, it's based on the premise that you must constantly be reaching for something unattainable in order to motivate yourself to act. The concept of potential represents a mistrust in your ability to self-motivate. The demand for potential is intended to be a pep talk to get us to move. The problem is that it actually can make us more passive because we know that reaching our potential is not possible. If we're demanding ourselves to reach our potential, and say we have four important roles in our life (student, relationships, art, health), then we're demanding 400% energy with only 100% to give. We're always falling short. And the notion that shooting beyond our reach is motivational misleads us to chronically evaluate whether we're reaching our potential or not which can foster more insecurity. We know we're trying to fool ourselves to strive for perfection but using tricks to self-motivate fosters mistrust in ourselves which elevates fear.

Work/life balance is another concept that eventually works against us. The intention is to be attentive to our overall wellbeing and not over-invest our identity in our work. It's a motivational strategy. Unfortunately, it can lead to frustration and resentment. Most of us live in a world where our demands exceed our resources of time and energy, making it impossible to attain a true level of work/life balance. So, when we strive for work/life balance, we become very sensitive to how unbalanced we are. We can judge ourselves negatively for not feeling balanced or become resentful of the world that won't allow it. So, again, we set a standard that we fear we can't attain and judge ourselves harshly when we fall short.

What is a different approach that keeps fear in its sweet spot and keeps values in the foreground? Instead of striving for passion and happiness, strive for purpose and meaning. For many, purpose and meaning connote the same thing. For others, purpose has more of a motivational dimension and meaning has more of a reflective dimension. If I strive for purpose, I bring my values into the foreground of my thinking without demanding any emotion like passion to be attached to it. There are many things we do that we don't like but have purpose for us. On days when acting on purpose brings good feelings with it like passion, then that's an added bonus not the determining factor of whether we're engaged in something right for us. Similarly, if I become more focused on finding meaning in the day rather than happiness, I am focusing on something deeper than just my current mood or emotion. I'm bringing my values into play by reflecting on activities that were meaningful to me. On days when that reflection also makes me happy, it's another bonus but not the new standard.

Instead of striving for potential, strive for expression. Striving for expression of your values is something we can control and draws energy from our values relationship rather than motivational tricks. Fear stays in the background and values lead. Challenges transition from being fear triggers to just a reality of living a life of purpose and meaning.

Instead of striving for balance, strive for harmony. At the beginning of each day, decide what you believe is the right devotion of your time and energy in relation to your life roles. You may feel that the right thing for you to do is to spend 90% of your time on one role, 5% on another, and 5% on another. The next day, wipe the slate clean and ask the same question. The answer may be the same or completely different. Sometimes you may only be able to spend 2% of your time, once a week on an important life role. That may not seem balanced, but you are harmonizing your values with other important components of your life. If each day, you are prioritizing your time and energy according to what you believe is most right, you are living in harmony with your values. If an orchestra strived to play in a balanced manner, the sound wouldn't capture the contrasts of each instrument nor movements of the music.

Paradoxically, the more we strive for purpose, meaning, expression, and harmony, the more we experience passion, happiness, balance, and optimal performance. It's attaining these experiences by effect instead of intention.

Strategy #6: Moving from Perceiving Outcomes as Life-critical "Have to's" to Life-enhancing "Want to's"

We all know that outcomes are important. Outcomes serve five positive purposes: (1) they can serve as an additional motivation to do something we find hard, unpleasant, or boring; (2) they serve as a reward for our hard work; (3) they provide feedback about our work; (4) they can create expanded opportunities for us in the future; and (5) we tend to feel positively evaluated by others when we attain outcomes. So, outcomes matter a lot. It's okay to want positive outcomes. And as long as outcomes remain a "want to" in our mental approach, they work for us. However, when outcomes shift from a "want to" to a "have to," they significantly get in the way of our optimal performance. If I have to have an outcome, then I cannot fail. If I cannot fail, then my fear of failure exponentially increases and I can slip into over-control or avoidance mode resulting in a plateau effect.

How do we keep outcomes in perspective amidst the pressure of needing outcomes to succeed in life? As noted in Chapter 3, the key is to move from a noun focus to a verb focus. Nouns are outcomes (e.g., grades, achievements, relationships), which we don't completely control. When we have the mindset of needing outcomes, we are very noun-focused. By contrast, verbs are what we do. They are our actions, which we have more control over. When we don't control something, we become more aware of uncertainty, which can increase fear. A verb focus keeps fear in perspective because it concentrates our energy and attention on our behavior instead of factors beyond our control.

In fact, you can limit your focus to just four verbs each day: *learning, expressing what you've learned, relating, and taking care of yourself*. At any given time of the day, one of these four verbs will be relevant. When you are working on a new project, work to learn not for achievement of outcome. When it's time to perform focus on expressing what you've learned and combining that with your talent. When interacting with others, focus on how you want to relate with the other person (e.g., with kindness, curiosity, respect). When we focus on the relationship instead of relating, we become very evaluative and constantly read how the other person is reacting to us. Concentrating on the verb of relating is one of the skills people with social anxiety use to interact more effectively with others despite feeling uncomfortable. And anytime during the day when you're not learning, expressing what you've learned, or relating, focus on taking care of yourself. Whenever you find yourself overwhelmed by nouns and outcomes, take a deep breath, and move into the most applicable verb.

There are several advantages to being verb-focused. First, it keeps fear in its proper perspective. Second, the more verb-focused you are, the more nouns you collect. You actually attain more outcomes because you're in an optimal mindset for high performance. There's a popular mantra about the importance of focusing on process versus outcome for high performance. That's partly true. It's not just process, though, it has to be a purposeful process. You must be engaged in a process that has true purpose and relevance for you in order to perform at your highest level. A third advantage is that hard work is more acceptable when you're verb-focused. When you're staying within yourself and engaged in purposeful work, you are more accepting of the hardness and stress that comes with it. When we're focused on nouns, we become overwhelmed with everything we have to control to get the outcomes. The difficulty of all we have to attend to and manage becomes less acceptable. Fourth, and most important, when we are verb-focused, we experience more joy when we actually attain outcomes. When we have to have an outcome and are noun-focused, the first emotion we experience when we attain that outcome is not joy, it's relief. When we're verb-focused, the success is in the work and outcomes are viewed as a bonus, icing on the cake. Remember, there is nothing wrong with wanting an outcome, it's needing it that gets in our way.

There are times when outcomes are front and center of a task. When you develop goals and objectives for a task, it's okay to include outcomes as a starting point. Then list everything that has to happen for that outcome to occur. After that full list is completed, cross off everything that is not within your control. The listed items left over are what we call Positioning

Goals. These are items that are within their control and best position them to make an A. Positioning Goals should be the primary focus. Giving attention to the other items on the list distracts from Positioning Goals and can negatively impact performance. Try this exercise the next time you feel a strong need for a particular outcome.

Step 5. Giving Voice to &: From Game Plan to Action

As the functional effectiveness of the Water Quality Division began to decrease despite a significant increase in resources and talent, the group scheduled a day-long retreat near the end of the fiscal year. They decided to take a historical perspective and look back at the history and evolution of their department. It became very clear that change had been very gradual and slow-paced over the course of the department's history. Necessary adjustments were very small and, therefore, did not spark fear among the small group. Expectations from the State were also a little below what the group's talent was, and so there was rarely any pressure and outcomes were usually pretty easily attainable. Fortunately, the initial group was made up of hard workers who gained meaning from good work, and they were successful in their eyes, as well as the State's.

But the recent sudden influx of resources, despite being a wonderful thing, was shocking and scary to the original group. Everything shifted suddenly, including expectations, which triggered fear. A great discussion around fear and ambiguity ensued. Individuals shared their personal experiences and how they managed these difficult emotions. They were able to connect many of their functional ineffectiveness to everyone managing fear, anxiety, and ambiguity in ways that were having an organizational impact. From avoidance, to over-control, to dichotomizing their reality into all-or-none thinking, it was all playing out in a way that became fascinating for the group to see once they stopped and used their analytical skills to understand the dynamics. After discussions loosened up, the team was able to talk more openly and problem solve.

The legacy staff of Aisha, Max, Julia, and Ron led the discussion by diagnosing the problem. Aisha, who had always been the division's main conduit between older and newer staff, addressed the issue, "I think we're missing some opportunities here." She pointed to the other legacy staff, "Back when we had a smaller budget, the four of us had to work efficiently together." She motioned to the other three, "We've worked together for over ten years." Ron, Julia, and Max nodded. "Now it's exciting to work on these new projects, but I think we're overlooking some functional growth that's been happening." Aisha looked back at Julia and asked, "Jules, what's my greatest strength?"

Julia immediately replied, "Communication. You know exactly what to say and when to say it."

"What about my weaknesses?" Aisha replied.

"You're unorganized. You know where things are, but it's a chaos no one can understand but you." Julia answered. "But that's why we would have Ron be team lead when a project had a lot of detailed parts."

Aisha smiled nodding her head as she looked back to the rest of the group, "You see the four of us got to the point where we didn't have to discuss how we'd delegate assignments. We worked as one – like a jazz band who've been playing together for years."

The group seemed to understand. Aisha looked at a new hire, Bethany, "Take Bethany, here. I worked with Bethany two weeks ago on a water table analysis and we worked so well together."

Bethany agreed stating, "Aisha knew exactly where to gather samples. It would have taken me twice as long."

"And you taught me that new hydropunch technique." Aisha looked from Bethany to the group,

"But I haven't been assigned to work with her since."

Nica spoke up, "I worked well with Ron on a project last month. He was able to contextualize data anomalies I was struggling with."

"And we're both morning people." Ron added, "I'm on a team now that likes to burn the midnight oil. I do my best work when the sun's coming up."

Aisha concluded, "We're starting to emulsify as a group but no one is keeping track or prioritizing these working relationships. As soon as a new project comes in, we're only arranging teams based on availabilities, initial interest, and expertise. We're too focused on the project and making changes for change's sake."

Aisha's point was undeniable. Over the next few months, she focused her work on tracking and organizing functional relationships between the division's staff. The work gained more and more traction which increased productivity, morale, and growth. Eventually, Aisha was named Chair of the Division and by the time she retired ten years later, the division had grown to 30 cohesive employees.

The organization was holding fear and ambiguity well. The sudden change that was scary for some and exciting for others was now managed through open communication and vulnerable exploration of difficult emotions stemming from uncertainty and ambiguity. Fear was being held well, creating a blend of functional effectiveness that honored the past, present, and future.

References

Crace, R.K., & Crace R.L. (2020). *Authentic Excellence: Flourishing and resilience in a Relentless World*. Routledge.

Greenberg, M. (2017). *The stress-proof brain: Master your emotional response to stress using mindfulness & neuroplasticity*. New Harbinger.

Kotter, J.P. (2014). *Accelerate. Building strategic agility for a faster-moving world.* Harvard Business Review.

Kotter, J.P., Akhtar, V., & Gupta, G. (2021). *Change: How organizations achieve hard- to – image results in uncertain and volatile times.* Wiley.

Kotter, J.P., & Cohen, D.S. (2002). *The heart of change: Real-life stories of how people change their organizations.* Harvard Business Review Press.

Schwartz, J.M. (2011). *You are not your brain: The 4-step solution for changing bad habits, ending unhealthy thinking, and taking control of your life.* Avery.

Schwartz, J.M., & Begley, S. (2002). *The mind and the brain: Neuroplasticity and the power of the mental force.* Regan Books.

Schwartz, J.M., & Beyette, B. (1997). Brainlock: Free yourself from obsessive-complusive behavior. Regan Books.

Scwhartz, J.M., Stapp, H.P., & Beauregard, M. (2004). The volitional influence of the mind on the brain, with special reference to emotional self-regulation. In Beauregard, M. (Ed.), *Consciousness, emotional self-regulation, and the brain* (pp. 195–238). John Benjamin.

7

PRODUCTIVE "&" FULFILLED

TRANSFORMATIVE OPTIMIZER: MEANINGFUL ACHIEVEMENT

The Easton Community Garden was an important hub for resources and neighborhood activities. Not only was the garden a valued green space in the middle of the city, the garden served as a venue for artists; offered classes that taught important skills; provided food from upstate farms; and served as a meeting ground for community planning.

Kent was the Executive Director of the nonprofit organization that ran the Easton Community Garden (ECG). He'd been the garden's founder. The person responsible from transforming the empty lot into a sustainable garden and community center that the neighborhood had come to rely on. Kent's personality was infectious. His optimism and connection to nature and people drew the neighborhood to the garden. There was no shortage of volunteers, activists, or community organizers during the first ten years of the ECG. Folks from the neighborhood made the garden into a vibrant center of community resources.

DOI: 10.4324/9781003265726-7

Step 1. Recognizing the Or Conflict: Productivity – Value or Need?

We've discussed the importance of values-led engagement, but once we're engaged, how do we pursue meaningful achievement? Organizations have an inherent motive toward effectiveness, and typically, effectiveness is defined as being productive. But how is productivity defined by organizations? What is optimal productivity?

Productivity is typically measured by outcomes. Because of the uncertainty that surrounds outcomes, an organization can drift to managing that uncertainty through perfectionistic expectations. The "bottom line" can become a fear-based need and when such expectations lead the culture, productivity becomes measured by a maximization principle. Productivity becomes measured by platitudes, such as reaching our potential or giving 110%. This mindset can create a demand for linear progress and causes every goal to be critical. Many organizations make everything task both important and urgent to where "crisis management" of goals becomes the norm. While this can result in high levels of productivity and output, there is a cost often seen as a lack of individual fulfillment, stress, and burnout. Performance metrics can outweigh the organization's commitment to its purpose – its "Why."

Conversely, a culture that focuses on fulfillment can be vulnerable to over-defining fulfillment by emotions or mood. Meaning and purpose can shift to whether we're feeling happy, content, and/or motivated. Platitudes such as "find your passion," "living the joy-filled life," and "striving for happiness" can start to gain cultural traction. Productivity can be interpreted as being devalued if it leads to upset feelings. Unmanaged difficult emotions can negatively impact productivity. In a competitive arena, fulfillment without productivity can lead to a loss of organizational viability.

Over the years, the neighborhood began to attract more and more people. Developers began to invest in commercial and residential projects. The community worried about Kent's perspective on the changes in the neighborhood.

Nichole, the organization's treasurer, expressed her concerns, "Kent, developers are working to rezone this block and our funding is drastically low. All the construction is causing more issues with rodents and it's getting more and more expensive to maintain the garden."

Kent responded, "I understand, but you can't focus on the negative. The garden is a place of hope – a reprieve for the community. We've been through hard times before and we'll get through them again.

"Not if we don't increase fund-raising initiatives immediately." Nichole argued.

"And lobby city officials to protect us from rezoning," Abby, a lawyer and member of the board, added.

"You have to believe in the community." Kent assured, "There will always be money worries and real estate threats, but you can't let it dictate your energy. The Easton Community Garden is about the neighborhood — the people. You can choose to put your energy into stress or you can put your energy into hope."

Step 2. Finding the Purpose of &: Meaningful Achievement

How do we find that optimal blend of high productivity & fulfillment? As mentioned in the introductory chapter, the Authentic Excellence Initiative defines flourishing as a consistent level of productivity, fulfillment, and resilience (Crace & Crace, 2020). Is there always tension between these dynamics, or can they be complementary? Can organizations develop and sustain a culture where productivity & fulfillment lead to flourishing? There are several steps that organizations can take to create an "&" culture through meaningful achievement. These include (1) revisiting platitudes, (2) finding the underlying values that are a part of productivity, (3) understanding optimal productivity at individual and organizational levels, and (4) understanding how stress is interpreted and manifested. From these steps, achievement starts to be viewed as something deeper than just performance.

Platitudes can often serve as driving themes and/or a vision for an organization. Platitudes serve to motivate, direct, and inspire. They can also be used to pass important organizational values through multiple generations. But platitudes can become sacred and impervious to challenge, particularly when the organization becomes known by its platitudes. They can become the measuring stick of how productivity and fulfillment are defined for all. Unintentionally, platitudes can create a culture of judgment, rigidity, and divisiveness. For instance, an employee may be a solid performer but if they don't ascribe to a company platitude, they can feel pressure to remain silent about that for fear of judgment. At worse, a solid performer might demonstrate a drop in performance and/or seek to disassociate or leave the organization. This can eventually impact morale, performance, and retention. To avoid this ineffective impact, platitudes should meet the test of reason, current reality, and action in measurable terms. They should connect to organizational values and have an inclusive impact. If a platitude is no longer reflective of the organizational values and/or creates a tension among members that negatively impacts productivity and fulfillment it is probably time to select a more impactful organizational platitude.

By devoting time and energy to operationalizing the *values* of the team and individuals, fulfillment is not only motivational but also measurable. Fulfillment comes from engaging in authentically held values. By assessing and crystallizing a team's values, you have found a means of measuring fulfillment. Goals can develop from values and productivity can stem from such goals. Values-centered goal setting sets the stage for meaningful achievement by providing motivation and direction but evokes a deeper sense of fulfillment by tapping into purpose.

Applying the *optimization* mindset to values-centered goals can also lead to more meaningful achievement. Goals defined according to a maximization principle can often create a level of psychological pressure that is more driven by fear than values and gets in the way of optimal performance. It also assumes the same direct linear relationship of output across individuals, whereas we know that individuals vary as to how much effort results in increased performance. The optimization principle assumes that values lead and pace is determined by meaningful achievement.

In order to find that right balance of productivity and fulfillment, it is also important to understand how the organizational culture views and manages *stress* in the context of productivity. What is the difference between what is stressful and what is straining in an organization's practices? Stress comes from the challenge of expressing values amidst uncertainty. Strain is when these values are expressed in an unhealthy manner or at a pace that is unsustainable. Norms can develop that either glorify stress, celebrate stress, or support each other amidst stress. *Stress glorification* often occurs when an organization is mostly comprised of highly talented individuals to where people start creating distinction by their effort. Stress glorification refers to norms that glorify hard for hard's sake and is a form of self-elevation. People can attach their self-worth to comparing their effort to others, constantly trying to one-up each other, and developing a badge of honor by how much they're suffering. This type of norm is unsustainable. *Stress celebration* is when a group is engaged in a worthy hard and when finished, they come together and reflect and celebrate the meaning of the work and the fact that they were able to do it together. *Stress support* is the support and encouragement we provide each other to acknowledge both the values behind the work and the difficulty of the work. How a group thinks about stress and manages it can determine whether productivity and fulfillment can be complementary.

Nichole and Abby were not going to let Kent's approach jeopardize ECG's viability. They got to work. Over the course of several months, Nichole and Abby organized a dozen fundraising parties; they started charging nominal fees for the classes offered in the garden; and they attended every city council meeting to monitor any threats developers might pose to the garden's lot. The tactics began to work. Funds were starting to reach a sustainable level. Several city council members were blocking any development that threatened the garden. And more newcomers to the neighborhood started to show up to classes and events. Newcomers that were able to pay more for classes.

Kent quietly stepped down as Executive Director. He was proud of the work he had done, but he felt ECG had turned into more of an organization than a neighborhood resource. Maybe that was necessary for the garden to survive and if that was true, he wasn't the person to lead the organization into the future.

Step 3. Analyzing Your Team – Finding the Meaning behind Achievement

Bringing Platitudes Down to Earth

- What are the mottos, themes, platitudes that are prominent in the organization?
- How are these platitudes communicated and reinforced?
- How and why did they originate?
- How old are they? How embedded are they in the fabric of the organization's history?
- How often are they discussed, revisited, or challenged?
- What is the impact, both positive and negative, of these platitudes on productivity and fulfillment?
- What values and fears may be driving these platitudes?

Values-Centered Goal Setting

- What are the prominent values of the team?
- What do those values look like when they are healthy in action and unhealthy in action?
- What productivity goals can be developed from these prominent team values?
- What are the prominent values of each team member and what goals can be developed from those values that are congruent with the organization's goals?

Optimizing Performance

- What is each team member's optimal level of effort and output?
- At what level of energy and effort does performance start to diminish?
- What are the implications of the individual variation of optimal effort for how the team approaches their work?
- What norms can be established around work environment that is inclusive and flexible around individual effort that still feels equitable and fair?

Differentiating Stress versus Strain

- How is stress glorified in the organization? How did that norm originate and how is it enabled?
- How is stress celebrated in a healthy manner? How routinized are these celebrations?
- What support practices exist for managing stress?

Abby took over as Executive Director. Nichole didn't mind Abby assuming the role, but she was concerned about the enterprising direction the garden was going. A year and a half prior ECG was in danger of folding due to Kent's idealistic approach. Now the organization was moving at a pace that lost sight of the garden's purpose — serving the community.

On a Saturday morning, Nichole was out walking her dog when she saw Michael and his mother. Michael was a teenager who had spent most of his childhood volunteering and attending every class the garden offered. Nichole caught up to Michael, "Hey, Michael! How have you been?" They greeted each other. Nichole asked, "I haven't seen you around the garden lately. Everything ok?"

"Yeah, things are fine." Michael answered politely.

Nichole tried a different angle, "They've had a bunch of carpentry classes at the garden lately. I thought I'd see you there. You used to love those classes."

Michael and his mother gave each other a look.

"What?"

Michael answered, "The classes are too expensive, Nichole."

"And you all don't do any neighborhood events anymore." Michael's mother added, "When was the last time you threw a potluck at ECG?"

"We've been trying to cut back on events because of liability issues." Nichole felt ridiculous repeating Abby's overly litigious reasoning.

Michael and his mother gave Nichole a disappointed look.

Step 4. Readying for &: Game Plan for Meaningful Achievement

Grounding Platitudes in Purpose

From the team analysis, take each platitude or theme that is prominent in the organization and create a large poster for each theme. Explicitly denote all dynamics that were identified to be a part of each platitude. How did it originate? What keeps it alive? How do people interpret its meaning? How has its meaning changed over time? What is the impact on the team, both positive and negative? What purpose and meaning is behind it? What fears are attached to it? What does it look like in action when it's healthy and unhealthy? Once the identified dynamics are laid out in full view, distinguish what of each platitude has true value, purpose, and meaning at this time of the organization and what is unnecessary. Develop actionable goals that emanate from the underlying purpose of the platitude rather than the platitude itself.

Nichole contacted Kent who hadn't been to the garden in months — not since a 100-year-old Oak was removed making room for more lucrative yoga classes. Abby had grown the nonprofit into a thriving business. Most of ECG's classes were patronized by folks who were not from the neighborhood. Nichole enlisted Kent to organize a counter initiative so that ECG could reclaim some of its original purpose.

Optimal Values Expression = Optimal Achievement

From the team analysis of values-centered goal setting, create a graph with an inverted U, bell-shaped curve for each organizational value. Label the X-axis (horizontal line) as "Values Expression," and the Y-axis (vertical line) as "Effectiveness." Label the left side of the curve as "Under-Attention," the middle of the curve as "Optimal Attention" and the right side of the curve as "Over-Attention." The inverted curve assumes that when a value is under-attended or over-attended, it negatively impacts effectiveness. On the graph, depict what each value looks like in action on all three points of the curve. This will illuminate when a value is being acted on as merely a preference or want (under-attention) or has drifted into a need (over-attention). Seeing each value depicted in this manner creates a deeper understanding of how values are being expressed in the organization and the impact such expression is having. The values that warrant the most work become evident, as well as the values that should be celebrated for their optimal expression. As the optimal expression of each value is clarified, develop specific goals that emanate from this optimal zone. Do this exercise for both group goals and individual goals. Have each team member clarify individual goals that optimally contribute to that value.

Faster at 85%

Elite sprinters have learned that sprinting at 100% effort results in a slower time because certain muscles are tensed that should be relaxed. They learn that sprinting at 80–90% effort results in being faster. At both an individual and organizational level, a deeper understanding of what optimal energy, effort, and expression should look like is critical for meaningful achievement. One of the most important developmental shifts for first-year college students is to effectively discern what optimal effort and engagement looks like for each of their classes. At first, fear and insecurity about academics at a higher level can cause them to believe they should study everything assigned at equal levels of depth. That maximizing mindset eventually becomes unsustainable and results in less effective performance. At first, it's much scarier to discern the varying degrees of effort and strategies that are applied to studying for each class, but courageously stepping into such discernment results in better performance. That's the essential difference between first-year and last-year students (at the undergraduate and graduate levels), they have learned to discern how to apply themselves optimally to academia. This dynamic can often happen with new members of an organization trying to make their mark compared to veterans of an organization who have developed a level of discernment.

Having open discussions positively impacts another component of group performance – it diminishes the "social loafing effect" (Hardy, 1990; Hardy & Latane, 1988; Latane, 1986; Latane, Williams, & Harkins, 1979; Williams, Harkins, and Latane, 1981; Williams, Nida, Baca, & Latane, 1989). Research has indicated that as the size of a group increases, the effort of each individual decreases proportionally due to a "hide in the crowd" effect. If an organization takes on the task of honoring the optimization principle but leaves it up to every individual to figure that out, an individual loafing or effort minimization effect can occur unintentionally. Having open discussions among team members is essential to find the right balance of individuals truly challenging themselves to work hard while discerning when the point of diminishing returns occurs. It gives people an opportunity to learn about each other from performance-based and values-centered perspectives. Someone could share that they do their best creative work in the mornings, that a particular value is what motivates them to step into hard work, and a particular platitude does nothing for them. Hearing from everyone starts to create an awareness of an organizational work climate that can be optimized.

Shifting from Stress Glorification to Stress Celebration & Support

It's important for an organization to clearly understand how stress may be glorified. Is there a constant one-upping of team members as to who is working harder? Is success defined by how much one is suffering? Do annual awards start to take the shape of the "sucks to be you" award because of extraordinary hardship that an employee faced? Stress glorification culture creates an environment where wellbeing is seen as competitive with excellence and maximal effort is espoused. It often leads to burnout, which negatively impacts fulfillment. While values and platitudes can often be the rationale for glorifying stress, it is really more rooted in fear and insecurity. Unmanaged fear can result in this over-controlling, perfectionistic perspective about achievement that eventually disrupts both productivity and fulfillment.

Instead, organizations should shift to seeing stress as a function of the values that drive their motivation. It requires effort to keep values-centered stress healthy. One approach to keeping stress healthy is to routinize the celebrations of the "why" behind the stress that the organization experiences. Develop norms of celebrating the conclusion of projects that were hard but values-aligned. Create awards that celebrate the values that are expressed and the goals that are achieved from those values. Celebrate when team members demonstrate the optimization principle and exemplify how wellness is essential to excellence. A second approach to fostering a healthy perspective of stress is to create explicit support systems. Creating a stress support culture develops the expectation that people will acknowledge hard work and encourage each other through difficult times, rather than one-upping each other. An organization can create "Flourishing Partners," to where pairs or small teams are formed with the intention of supporting each other around flourishing concepts. They encourage each other when things are difficult, challenge each other when motivation is lagging, keep each other mindful of the "why" of their work, and affirm success being defined by engagement in values-centered goals.

Step 5. Giving Voice to &: From Game Plan to Action

After much planning and organizing, a date was set for a community meeting. Folks from the neighborhood packed the garden along with local city officials, media, and community leaders.

They all voiced concerns:

"The purpose of ECG is to serve the community. The garden is no longer doing that." Kent and other people from the neighborhood vocalized.

Abby and other board members countered, "Having no funds to maintain the garden leaves it disrepair and vulnerable to rezoning. That doesn't serve the community either."

Michael pointed out, "So can we all agree that serving the community — the whole community — is the purpose of this garden?" Folks nodded in agreement.

Nichole added, "Well then we need to define the parameters of what 'serving the community' means. Then we can discuss when we cross the line and compromise that meaning."

Kent sniped, "When classes are $20 bucks a pop! That doesn't serve the community."

"When funds are so low, we can't even afford rodent traps." Abby snapped back.

Folks began to pile on:

"When artist can't afford the venue space."

"When trees are getting cut down."

"When we're sued into oblivion because we can't afford liability insurance."

When the heated declarations started to die down, Nichole spoke up, "Ok! I've listed every point made. Now it's time to come up with some rules and compromises."

It took several more meetings, but eventually rules were established so that the operations of the Easton Community Garden reflected the needs and concerns of the entire community:

- Monthly community events will be organized and open to the public. A certificate of insurance will be purchased for every event.
- Only one third of the courses offered will cost $20 per class. The other classes will be donation based or on a sliding pay scale. Anyone in the neighborhood experiencing financial hardship will be allowed to attend classes for free.
- All current trees and plant life in the garden will be maintained
- More hours will be allotted for garden maintenance. These hours will be centered around free agricultural and horticultural classes to encourage more volunteers.

- Every board member will participate in grant writing as well as recruiting more volunteers to apply for grants to fund the garden.
- Monthly meetings with city officials will be established to monitor neighborhood real estate development.
- Every quarter there will be another community meeting where folks will review and amend operational guidelines.

References

Crace, R.K., & Crace, R.L. (2020). *Authentic Excellence: Flourishing and Resilience in a Relentless World.* Routledge.

Hardy, C.J. (1990). Social Loafing: Motivational loses in collective performance. *International Journal of Sport Psychology, 21*: 305–327.

Hardy, C.J. & Latane, B. (1988). Social loafing in cheerleaders: effects of team membership and competition. *Journal of Sport & Exercise Psychology, 10,* 109–114.

Latane, B. (1986). Responsibility and effort in organizations. In P. Goodman (Ed.), *Groups and organizations,* (pp. 277–303). San Francisco: Jossey-Bass.

Latane, B., Williams, K.D., & Harkins, S.G. (1979). Many hands make light the work: The causes and consequences of social loafing. *Journal of Personality and Social Psychology. 37,* 822–832.

Williams, K.D., Harkins, S.G., & Latane, B. (1981). Identifiability as a deterrent to social loading: Two cheering experiments. *Journal of Experimental Social Psychology, 40,* 303–311.

Williams, K.D., Nida, S.A., Baca, L.D. & Latane, B. (1989). Social loafing and swimming: Effects of identifiability and relay performance of intercollegiate swimmers. *Basic and Applied Social Psychology, 10,* 73–81.

8

EMOTIONAL "&" ANALYTICAL

TRANSFORMATIVE OPTIMIZER:
INCLUSIVE 3D DECISION MAKING

"That's not how you run a business." Steve, the new owner of Bell's Bar, barked at Jason, the General Manager.

"Steve, these guys worked through the entire pandemic making no money. They deserve the best shifts now that we're back to full capacity."

"Not if it means they're flirting with overtime every week."

"Lou didn't mind paying overtime now and then. Oscar and John do all the little things to keep the place together."

"I don't care. That's not how you run a business."

Jason thought about quitting more often than he preferred. He had been the GM for Bell's Bar over the past six years, but during the pandemic, the old owner, Lou, sold the bar to Steve, a CPA looking to try his hand at the bar business. Lou had been an owner Jason could work with. He had allowed Jason to manage the staff in a way that prioritized employees' wellbeing. If workers were burnt out, he gave them time off. If workers needed more shifts, he amended schedules. If workers had insights into how to build clientele, he listened and implemented changes.

DOI: 10.4324/9781003265726-8

When Steve bought the bar, Jason was initially encouraged by how hands-off Steve was. As long as Jason, entered wages and sales on time and in the manner Steve preferred, there seemed to be no issues. Initially, Jason had more autonomy over bar than he had when Lou owned Bell's. Even though Lou supported most all Jason's management decisions, Jason still needed to explain the reasoning behind his decisions, and how those reasons benefited the wellbeing of the bar and its staff.

When Oscar's brother, John, moved to the US and needed work, Jason hired him. Lou supported the idea. Oscar was a hardworking, long-time employee and providing his family with an opportunity was a worthy endeavor. Lou asked Jason to regularly check in to see how John was dealing with the learning curve and if there was anything they could to do to provide support. After a year, John had become one of Bell's fastest bartenders.

On a Monday afternoon the new owner, Steve, called Jason into his office. "I want you to switch Stacey to Wednesday nights and John to Friday nights."

Jason was confused responding, "She can't. She has school on Wednesdays."

"Well, if she can't work Wednesdays, we don't have a spot for her. My business has nothing to do with her education."

Jason tried to ignore the harshness of Steve's deductions. He had learned that Steve would only listen to facts and numbers. "Why do you want to move her off of Fridays?"

"Her sales numbers are low."

Jason breathed a sigh of relief. This was a misunderstanding he could easily explain in bar math. "Those numbers don't reflect the bartenders' actual sales. They share registers all the time when it's busy." Steve looked at him blankly. Jason continued, "The bar makes a lot more money when bartenders are focused on shelling out drinks instead of ringing transactions under their particular employee number."

"Well, they need to start ringing under their own numbers. I need to track employee performance."

"But that will slow down sales when we're slammed." Jason argued, "Like a lot."

"Well then you'll have to find bartenders that can ring in transactions properly without slowing down."

Jason tried to think of an analytical counterpoint, "Modern register systems have easier ways to track individual employee sales. We need a newer system anyway, remember? This one's 15 years old and crashes all the time."

"Too expensive."

Jason searched for an argument before stating bluntly, "You will lose money by doing this."

Steve could've explained his thinking. That he didn't think the change would substantially affect sales because while the bartenders might not make as many transactions per peak hour, the customers were still likely to remain in the bar and drink the same number of drinks over the course of two hours. This would extend the amount of time the bar looked busy which could improve the bar's reputation as a popular spot. If Steve had asked for Jason's experiential input, he might have been able to modify his theory more accurately. But if he demonstrated any doubt in his thinking, the chance of Jason not following his directives increased. Steve was convinced that bar sales would go up because he was trimming the fat and implementing ideas that prioritized business. He didn't have the time or energy to manage someone challenging his plan.

Bell's Bar had always managed impressive sales. The original owner, Lou, had leased the right location at the right time ten years prior. And the fortunate sales that allowed Lou to prioritize staff needs over sales efficiency now allowed Steve the flexibility to test his business tactics. If his methods didn't work or if staff quit, there was an ample pool of service industry workers and a steady stream of customers. He felt he had to be seen as decisive; he believed in his strategy and was afraid that seeking input from Jason would look insecure or inept. He needed to show strength and conviction. Besides, despite being a really smart GM, Steve felt Jason led with his heart too much. He felt his "logical" arguments were more smokescreens for what he wanted emotionally.

The staff was angry when Jason explained the procedural changes. Not only were these changes unnecessary, but it caused the bartenders to make less tips. They complained and Jason empathized. "Listen, I hate it too. And I know it's getting tougher and tougher to work here, but I need this job." He appealed to the group, "Many of you need this job, and even with these stupid changes we make more money here than we would at other bars in town."

Jason's mind immediately flashed to an image of him tossing and turning in bed tonight. Issues like this hit Jason hard. He was sensitive. In fact, most of his childhood he was labeled as "too sensitive." He even believed that *his sensitivity was a weakness. Issues that touched his emotions seemed to affect him deeper and longer than others. And once he was moved emotionally, he had trouble turning his mind off. It typically resulted in one or two sleepless nights before he found a perspective that his mind would allow him to sleep. Today, he felt the full weight of the responsibility of every staff member, yet none of the power to fix the problem.*

What does Jason and the staff do to endure; to strategically influence change; and work with an unbending owner?

Step 1. Recognizing the OR Conflict: What Leads Most – Head or Heart?

Unfortunately, organizations, such as Bell's Bar, with rigid, unbending leaders and employees who can't afford to leave are more commonplace than they should be. Often times, when dealing with conflicts, credibility can be ascribed to logical analysis over emotional sensitivity, or vice-versa. While everyone has the capacity to be analytical and emotionally sensitive, we tend to develop preferences that become habitual over time. In an organization, value and credibility is usually based on power rather than majority. The ascribed value of logical analysis or emotional sensitivity often flows from the leader's preferences and is usually evident in decision-making and what arguments are valued by the leader. Steve gave less value to Jason's arguments because he felt they were based on emotional factors, even though Jason was presenting his arguments with a logical narrative.

During times of transition and uncertainty, fear and insecurity can lead which can in turn amplify the ascribed value of logic OR emotion. The result is greater rigidity, an over-idealizing of staff that align with that preference, and a devaluing of those who are on the other end of the continuum. In other words, there becomes an over-attribution of someone's value based simply on their preferential habit of logic or emotion.

Rigidity is Always Emotional Even when Wrapped in Logic

The transition to a new owner at Bell's Bar created a lot of uncertainty for everyone. But Steve had the power. He also had needs that were stemming from insecurity and fear. He needed to prove himself as a restaurateur. He had taken a risk to venture out of his comfort zone as a CPA. His analytical abilities had served him well in academia and the accounting industry. He had excelled. He had also found himself bored in the past few years. He dreamed of something exciting and challenging. When the opportunity came along that could test his entrepreneurial spirit, he took the leap. But not without great concern expressed from his family. He needed this to work to assure him and others that he had made the right decision. He was going to do it his way, and that way was to stay with the data.

Steve's fear-based need was a reasonable response to his circumstance. But his management of that need was an over-reliance and singular focus on an ability that had been successful for him in the past. Of course, it makes sense as to why he would start with that approach – 'go with what you know.' But fear-based need creates rigid thinking. He became myopic in his thinking and used his positional authority to demand an approach from others. Because he had discounted Jason as being too emotional, he missed valuable information that could have helped him run his business. Ironically, his fear was causing him to be less logical while at the same time demanding it: when rigidity seeps into the fabric of decision-making, emotions become the driver. The more there is a divide among what is valued and an Or takes hold between logic and emotion, the more an organization is being guided by unmanaged emotions, no matter the packaging. Emotions are wonderful things, just like logical thoughts, but they both require management.

Step 2. Finding the Purpose of &: Inclusive 3D Decision-Making

Why should organizations give greater credibility and value to the integration of logic and emotion? In a linear world, one can get away with rigidly affixing to logic or emotion, following the path of myopic thinking. But we live in a nonlinear world, which requires critical, creative, and whole-brain thinking. Flourishing organizations practice a similar approach that occurs in the transition from secondary school education to higher education. In secondary school, students are taught A & B and are tested on A & B. In higher education, students must learn A & B but then extrapolate from that learning to be tested on F & G. That requires critical and creative thinking. Rote memory, emotional rigidity, and/or singular processing just isn't sufficient in today's world.

But what if an organization highly values both thinking and feeling? It opens the opportunity for holistic decision-making that is inclusive of both creative and critical thinking, keeping values central. Emotions are critically important to our perceptions of the world around us. Sometimes emotions are the first to recognize that something is shifting around us before we fully comprehend what is happening. Emotions can be our first forms of awareness. To dismiss or devalue that important part of our brain function is to severely limit our ability to work effectively with complexity. But emotions need to be managed. We are not advocating that all decisions should be based on whatever ideas stem from emotions. But we are advocating paying attention. *Essentially, emotions serve as important reasons to pay attention and think more deeply.* This is not easy or natural. When we have strong emotions, we can act or judge in some manner. Think of the term "react." When we experience something that evokes emotions, it compels us to re-act, internally and externally. That initial reaction may or may not be congruent with our values and/or what is needed in a particular context.

Conversely, limiting our decisions to only data can limit our experience of context and can drift us away from our values. Remember, values are powerful because they are a part of our emotional, analytical, cultural, and experiential selves. To restrict ourselves only to logic can result in an unintentional drift away from values. Tuning only into logic is actually a form of tuning out. And sometimes that's the point. For many who strongly rely on logic, tuning into their emotions can be overwhelming because it introduces ambivalence and that nasty "What if..." question. We have a natural desire to clean up the messiness of push-pull emotions. So, we can see why it is natural for people who rely on logic to use analysis to control the messiness around them. In the same way, it is natural for emotionally sensitive people to "trust their intuition" to manage messiness. Both approaches are natural... and limiting. Emotions without the time for deeper thought and reflection can lead to hasty, reactive decisions. Analysis without tuning into emotions ignores critical context. Tuning in, honoring, and paying attention to what is felt, and giving time to think more deeply takes us to a deeper levels of decision-making that is creative, multi-dimensional, and values-centered. The challenge: It's hard to do; it requires intentionality and a shift in how we think about "mindset." The good news: This is one of the dialectic &s that is easier to enact as an organization than as an individual. In an organization, you can usually count on having people that reflect the full continuum of logic and emotion rather than experiencing the full continuum as an individual. As long as the full continuum is valued and respected in an organization, then inclusive decision-making ensues. In addition, by embracing the full continuum of both logic and emotion, you stay more aligned with values, instead of fear, because values require tuning into both emotions and analytical thinking. This creates the 3D effect of giving voice to values, emotions, and thoughts. In essence, the work is respecting and valuing the full continuum of thoughts and emotions through a concept known as "*deliberate compassion*," which aligns thoughts and emotions to purpose and values. Deliberate compassion allows an organization to move beyond the perceived safe harbor of cognitive or emotional rigidity that is evidenced when an OR culture is created and nurtured.

Step 3. Analyzing Your Team – Which "Too" Are You?

There are both formal and informal ways of assessing the continuum of logical analysis and emotional sensitivity for a team. Assessments such as the Myers-Briggs Type Indicator (Briggs & Briggs Myers, 2015) or the Keirsey Temperament Assessment (2018) assess preferential habits as it relates to the Thinking & Feeling continuum. Such assessments can provide helpful information for both individuals and as a team aggregate. Under skilled facilitation, they can stimulate engaging conversations among colleagues to enhance the understanding and appreciation of the full continuum.

More informally, a quick survey of the following three questions can prove to be a useful starting point for an organization to gain an appreciation of the continuum.

1. When it's time to make a final decision on something, do you mostly base that decision on logic and analysis, emotions and intuition, or a balance of both?
2. Where would most people, who know you well, put you on the continuum of logic and emotion?
3. Has anyone ever described you as "too sensitive," "too emotional," "too logical or analytical," or "too data driven?"

The Rare Combination that Is Becoming Less Rare

Individuals may be emotionally sensitive and not very analytical; or highly analytical and not very emotionally sensitive. But there are some individuals who are both. They are emotionally sensitive and highly analytical. We refer to them as active-minded, active-hearted individuals. Active-Minded, Active Hearted (AM/AH) individuals are emotionally attuned to themselves and their surroundings. When they are moved emotionally, they think deeply about their experience. These individuals can have trouble dismissing emotionally challenging experiences until their feelings and thoughts are resolved. Their range of emotional capacity allows them to experience profound beauty and joy in life, but it also can contribute to experiences of profound pain.

More attention has been paid in recent years to understanding the power and gift of sensitivity and vulnerability (Aron, 1997; Brown, 2012; Neff, 2011). Often AM/AH individuals are aware of their heightened sensitivity at a very young age. As children, they feel acutely aware of details, and pick up on emotions around them before others seem to. And because they are children, they are often overwhelmed by their sensitivity. They may also receive feedback from others that they are "too sensitive" or are made to feel like their sensitivity is a weakness. Based on those experiences, sensitive children may seek to suppress their sensitivity through over-control or avoidance, and entrench the Fear-Based Model of Excellence into their pattern of living. But suppressing one's authentic gift of sensitivity through over-control and avoidance is not sustainable.

An avoidant coping pattern AM/AH individuals may fall into is excessive substance use or unhealthy soothing. The intensity of being sensitive and analytical begs for relief. The most instant forms of relief are food, drugs, sex, pain, and compelling entertainment. So it is natural to seek these out for reprieve because they can quickly change brain chemistry. While such types of relief or "substances" can provide temporary avoidance-comfort, they can also be difficult to moderate and can become problems in and of themselves. AM/AH individuals can also exhibit controlling and perfectionistic behaviors to deal with the pressures of being emotionally sensitive and analytical. Chronic worry and intensity are common inhibitors for AM/AH individuals. This is why in the context of an organization, it can be easier to experience the full continuum of logic and emotion as a group rather than an individual.

Avoidance and over-control patterns of coping can turn into attributes that AM/AH individuals over-identify with. This identification can mislead one into thinking part of what makes them unique is their suffering, avoidance, or perfectionism. Identity misconceptions can be reinforced when a community builds around such identities. The fear-based coping patterns of dealing with AM/AH challenges can be seen as what is unique about a person instead of the beauty and power of being sensitive and analytical. Not only does suppressing sensitivity and analysis take an unsustainable mental and physical toll, it also prevents one from experiencing the benefits of being sensitive and analytical. AM/AH individuals can be powerfully empathic to the world and others. They can see opportunities for expression through avenues that may not be visible to most people. They can develop insights and communicate original ideas that strongly resonate with others. When AM/AH individuals develop the benefits of their sensitivity and analysis instead of suppressing them, they can experience powerful flourishing. The goal is to honor and embrace this expanded range of emotional and cognitive ability while managing the amplified pain and intensity in a healthy manner. The stress management and wellness strategies discussed in Chapter 4 and values work can help such individuals find that optimal level of healthy emotional management.

Whether it is from formal assessment or conversations about the continuum of logic and emotions, it is important for the team to have an open dialogue about what is learned about the individuals and the team as a whole. The key is to keep the focus on decision-making. It is easy for the conversation to drift into over-characterizing someone based on their sensitivity or analytical behavior. Individuals may have a lot of feelings and thoughts about particular issues, but when push comes to shove and it's time to decide or act, where on the continuum do they tend to fall? Understanding the group from this dynamic helps keep the focus on behavior and values rather than judgment about what a person should think or feel.

Step 4. Readying for &: Deliberate Compassion & Rethinking "Mindset"

Rethinking "Mindset"

When we ask individuals to define "mindset," the most common answer is "what you are thinking." This is true to some extent but it's misleading. Consider the following: Think of an upcoming event that is important to you. First, what do you hope to *experience* when you engage in that event? What are your *emotions* about this event? What are your *thoughts* about this event? What do you want your *focus* to be when you engage in that event?

If you could distill that focus into just a few words, what would they be? Finally, what values are being fulfilled by engaging in this event?

When we teach the concept of mindset as it pertains to flourishing, we are referring to an intentional focus at the point of engagement. When mindset is viewed in the more familiar definition of thoughts, our full range of thoughts (including conflicting ones) and the emotions that evoke further thoughts can be overwhelming and exhausting. Instead, we want to acknowledge and honor the wide range of thoughts and feelings but at the point of engagement, it's important to focus our minds on something that is true and purposeful to us.

Let's take a graduate entrance exam, such as MCATs, for example. A student may have had a lifelong dream to be a physician because of her love of science and helping people. She has worked hard her entire academic career to position herself for entry into medical school. Her grades are outstanding but not stellar enough to guarantee admission and so she believes doing well on her MCATs is critical. What she hopes to experience is a prepared mind and stellar scores. The values of her taking the exam are Achievement, Concern for Others (because she wants to help others as a physician), and Objective Analysis (her value of science). The emotions she has around this event are nervousness, fear, excitement, at times insecurity, and at times confidence. Her thoughts are about the material she has learned for the test, thoughts of assurance that she has prepared, and the nagging "what if...?" question. But, at the time of engaging in the event, she wants her focus to be on the material and trusting her mind to access the answer. Distilled, her mindset is going to be "Focus on the question in front of you and tell them what you know." This mindset allows for the full human experience of an event that is of high importance, while still bringing the mind back to what is most important in the moment. In this case, "Focus on the question in front of you and tell them what you know," keeps the mind where it needs to be despite all of surrounding noise of thoughts and feelings.

In the same manner, it is not only okay but it is encouraged for staff to have the full range of emotions and thoughts about aspects of their work and their relationships with each other. It's encouraged for people to honor their authenticity as to their values and their place on the continuum of logic and emotion. And when it comes to the point of engaging with others and engaging in decision-making, what do we want the focus point or mindset to be? For inclusive decision-making, it's deliberate compassion.

The Mindset of Deliberate Compassion

The mindset of Deliberate Compassion is not complex, it's just hard to do. Deliberate compassion has three components:

1. Deliberately focusing first, on the value a person brings to the team, and second, on the challenges a person brings to the team.
2. Deliberately leading with the value I bring to the team and working to manage the challenges that I bring to the team. Deliberate compassion places primary importance on what is most right for the moment, as opposed to the prominent emotion or thought of the moment. We can feel and think a wide range of things about a person or event, but in that moment, if we can deliberately set our mind on the value that someone brings and the values that are a part of the moment, a deeper level of engagement and open-mindedness occurs. It doesn't deny the challenges that a person brings and the frustration that may be a part of working with those challenges, but it keeps the mind focused on what is most important at that moment.
3. The mindset of deliberate compassion also entails one of the essential themes of this book: prioritizing values over fear.

When we are values-centered and managing fear well, we are much more likely to have an open mind and honor the full continuum of logic and emotion in ourselves and others. So, the distilled mindset (focus point) can be "Lead with values, hold fear well." It keeps our mindset clear and honest by honoring the reality of uncertainty around anything important, instead of platitudes like "be fearless." By engaging in deliberate compassion, we enjoy the vast creativity and critical thinking that a group brings to the table, it keeps decisions laser focused on values, and it allows people to be fully engaged, while emotional and thoughtful.

Step 5. Giving Voice to &: From Game Plan to Action

Steve couldn't sleep. As the sky slowly started to change color, he finally got up, turned on his gas fireplace in the living room, and sat on his couch staring at the flames. That is how he felt his career as a restaurateur was going — up in flames. It had been several months since he and Jason had argued about the schedule. He had been convinced his plan was the best plan. He had the data to prove it. And he was fine to let anyone leave who didn't like it. He had plenty of people to replace them, that was the beauty of the restaurant industry. "You don't like how I run things? Next." But that hadn't worked out so well. A couple of people eventually left and he replaced them immediately. But the new employees didn't like his style either so they quit. The next round of hires took much longer to fill. He felt like the people he interviewed spent more time asking him questions about work conditions than he did interviewing them. Some actually turned down the job after he offered it to them. Things were shifting. He was now short-staffed and it was starting to become evident by how often customers were complaining. Sales were declining. He could no longer assume an endless supply of staff or customers. He didn't like admitting mistakes, but the data was now clear, there were some flaws in his plan. While it made him nauseas to consider talking with Jason and seeking his input for fear of what Jason might think of him, he decided that was better than to see the bar fail and show his family that he really couldn't hack it as an entrepreneur.

Jason couldn't sleep. A few hours prior, Oscar, a close friend he'd worked with for six years, told Jason that he was leaving Bell's. He had been looking for other work for a few months and had just found something. He had told Jason that he just couldn't stand working for Steve anymore. Jason had tried his best to buffer Steve and his decisions from the staff, but the dominoes were falling and he didn't see the bar lasting under Steve's ownership for more than a few more months. He couldn't stop thinking about the lives that were affected by Steve's decisions during a critical time in the world's recovery from a pandemic. Either people stayed and were absolutely miserable and unhealthy; left without any guarantee of somewhere else to work; or like Oscar, searched until they found something else. Maybe Jason needed to start thinking about a new direction himself. "I'm obviously not cutting it as a GM." He took everyone's departure personally. He saw it as a failure on his part not being able to retain them. But he had been down this insomnia-driven, train of thought before. Another career path would require significantly more education, expense, and training. He felt trapped. Eventually, his mind started to strategize ways to talk with Steve when he shared the news about Oscar quitting. He wasn't hopeful but it was worth a shot. The phone rang. It was Steve.

They met for lunch at restaurant on the other side of town from Bell's Bar. Steve awkwardly let Jason know that he wanted to hear some of Jason's ideas about how to improve things at the bar. Jason shared some ideas with Steve and for the first time, Steve seemed receptive. But Jason didn't just share **his** ideas. He encouraged Steve to reach out to other bar owners, get to know his fellow entrepreneurs. It surprised Steve that Jason regarded him as an entrepreneur instead of an accountant playing bar owner. For the first time, he didn't feel like he needed to prove himself to Jason. They could work together; he could learn from Jason and others without seeming inept. Steve still felt like he needed to prove something to himself and his family, but was that shell was starting to crack?

That night, Steve remembered a university professor at the accounting firm who had conducted a seminar on the Myers-Briggs. He hadn't put much stock in distilling someone down to a 4-letter type, but he did find it somewhat interesting and was surprised at how accurately it had described some of his colleagues. He didn't like it, but it had also pretty accurately described him, too. He called Jason and asked his opinion about bringing this person in to do something similar for the bar staff.

A couple of weeks later, the entire team went through a morning seminar about preferences and habits and how those can be described according to typologies. They all took the MBTI and discussed the results as a group. Of the various types they discussed, the most interesting feature was where people fell on the Thinking-Feeling dimension. While there were some that were on the extreme ends of the continuum, including Steve on the far end of Thinking, most were in the mid-range. Most of the staff placed a high level of importance on both emotions and analysis when it came to decision-making. This surprised Steve. He had assumed that everyone would have been on the far end of the Feeling dimension. But that was because relative to him, everyone seemed to be too far on the Feeling end.

Equally fascinating, although somewhat uncomfortable, was when they were asked to each share the influences that may have shaped their place on the continuum. Steve realized that his upbringing had a lot to do with why he was so analytical and focused on data. As he connected those dots, he realized that emotional experiences had actually been important in shaping his love of objective analysis. Jason had been intrigued when the facilitator described the Active-Minded/Active-Hearted type and was embarrassed when everyone had said in unison, "Oh man, you just described Jason." But it was helpful for Jason to hear his sensitivity described as a gift and a strength, rather than a weakness. It was nice to hear how fortunate the team was to have Jason's gift of sensitivity, rather than the narrative he had heard most of his life of being "too sensitive."

When Steve asked the facilitator how they could make the best use of these results, the professor replied that it's not complex it's just hard to do. "Simply put," he said, "there needs to be a genuine respect and appreciation for the diversity that exists on this continuum of Feeling and Thinking. Everyone needs to feel seen and heard when they want to express their thoughts and feelings on a matter. Everyone knows that Steve is the boss, but it's important to take advantage of the thoughtfulness, creativity, and sensitivity that exists here." The professor turned directly to Steve, "When a decision needs to be made, you're certainly a smart enough guy to make a good decision. But consider taking the time to seek others' thoughts and feelings about it, you may find something worth considering. That also starts to build trust with the staff in your decisions. Even if they don't agree with it, they have a better chance of respecting it because they know you have considered several viewpoints. By valuing where everyone is on the continuum, you are honoring what they bring that is of value, rather than bemoaning that they are not more like you." The professor turned back to the group, "Because there are several people on staff who value tuning into their emotions, it's important for everyone to take the responsibility of managing their emotions in a healthy way. If you like, we can spend a few minutes near the end of our seminar to discuss healthy coping and self-care strategies. It really comes down to everyone committing to a mindset of healthy relating and honoring the value that everyone brings to the table, even amidst the absurd world of the service industry. What can each of you own as a responsibility to make this a healthy place to work? Try to boil it down to just a few words and share that with each other."

The following two quarters showed an increase in both sales and retention. In fact, a couple of former employees returned, including Oscar, because they had heard about the shift in work culture. Steve had connected with several restaurant and bar owners in the area and even hosted several events where guest speakers share industry ideas with each other. He realized he had a love of connecting with creatives and was finding himself to be more creative the more open he had become to others' ideas. At the end of these industry events, a fellow owner pulled Steve aside and told him she was opening another restaurant in the area and looking for a couple of additional partners. Would he be interested? Steve said he knew just the right person to consider as an additional partner.

Jason was helping one of the new employees prep the bar when John called from the office, "Jas, it's Steve, he wants to run something by you."

References

Aron, E.N., & Aron, A. (1997). Sensory-processing sensitivity and its relation to introversion and emotionality. *Journal of Personality and Social Psychology*, 73(2), 345–368. https://doi.org/10.1037/0022-3514.73.2.345

Briggs, K., & Briggs Myers, I. (2015). *The Myers-Briggs Type Indicator*. The Myers & Briggs Foundation.

Brown, B. (2012). *Daring greatly: How the courage to be vulnerable transforms the way we live, love, parent and lead*. Gotham Books.

Keirsey Temperament Assessment. (2018). Keirsey Temperament Assessment [online], https://keirsey.com/temperament-overview/

Neff, K.D. (2011). *Self-compassion: The proven power of being kind to yourself*. Harper Collins.

9

MENTORING "&" FOLLOWING

TRANSFORMATIVE OPTIMIZER: RECIPROCAL INFLUENCE

"Maria, do you have your outline for the dynamics section of your dissertation?"

"Well... no, Gwen, I actually started writing the section—"

"With no outline!" Everyone in the department ignored Gwen's volume. "Maria, you can't keep writing freely without a plan. Remember, I'm expecting 45 pages by Monday."

"I've already written 30 pages." Maria couldn't understand why Gwen overlooked her consistent production.

"You're not going to have any time to edit that sloppy first draft by Monday. You need a plan, Maria. You need thorough outlines before you start writing."

"Right, but I was inspired by the research and wanted to fall into the work."

"Maria, listen to me, I didn't get where I am today by just 'falling into the work.' You gotta plan. You gotta organize. Look at your desk." Maria's desk was scattered with stacks of paper. The stacks looked haphazard to Gwen, but Maria knew which reference materials and notes belonged to

DOI: 10.4324/9781003265726-9

which stack. Gwen shuffled through Maria's stacks of papers continuing, "This is a mess."

"I didn't want to interrupt my momentum. I was on a roll."

"It's not just the stacks of notes. Look at your cubicle." Maria looked around trying to guess what Gwen was getting at. "You don't have any pictures of loved ones. No awards. No interests. No sports teams. There's nothing here. No personalized touch whatsoever."

"I'm not a big sports person." Maria responded. "And I'm not close with my family."

"Well, it gives off the wrong impression. Like you're planning on leaving at any moment."

Maria was tired of Gwen's determinations, "It never occurred to me."

"Look at Stephanie's desk." Maria turned to the cubicle across the office. "She's got several pictures of family and friends; her diplomas – look how organized her papers are – she's even got a dream board." Gwen looked back a Maria. "You two are my protégés and I want you both to succeed."

Maria hated when Gwen referred to her as a protégé or compared her to Stephanie. Maria had more publications and better course evaluations than Stephanie, but Gwen always favored Stephanie's approach. "I understand," Maria relented.

"Now I want you to write 60 new pages with a full outline."

"You want me to write an outline even though I'm done writing the section?"

"The sooner you learn, the less backtracking you'll have to do. In fact, let's make it 70 pages."

Maria turned back to her work waiting for Gwen to leave.

In the coming months Maria played Gwen's game. She taped a picture of a luxury car on the wall with a caption that read 'Dream Car;' bought a hat with the local football team's logo and hung it on the corner of her cubicle; placed an old photo of her and her brother – whom she hadn't called in months – on her desk; and spent aggravating amounts of time creating outlines that hindered rather than helped her writing.

"There you go, Maria. Now you're coming around." Gwen remarked on Maria's performative progress.

Gwen's boot-camp style of mentorship combined with her one-track way of doing things had almost been enough to make Maria quit. She didn't. Maria earned her PhD and left Gwen's "one-way" mentorship in the past.

Step 1: Recognizing the Or Conflict: Mentoring Or Following

Most organizations have both formal and informal programs for mentoring. Many organizations believe that success is dependent on effective mentoring and as a result develop formal mentoring programs. Effective following, while helpful in terms of the success of organizations, is often attributed to great mentoring. The assumption is that if we create effective mentoring, we will by default have effective followers. Furthermore, it is often assumed that if followers increase their effectiveness, they will be selected to become mentors themselves. Any tensions that exist between the organizational dynamics of mentoring and following are either ignored or managed by over-attending to one role over the other.

When organizations approach mentoring or following as singular roles, they can create a one-way path of influence where mentors give and followers take what they are given. This limits the relationship between mentor and follower due to the power dynamics like experience, age, role, position, etc. The result is that most organizations end up assigning value to the role of mentor as opposed to the role of follower. It is, therefore, not surprising that members of organizations prefer mentoring over following. To be chosen as a mentor signifies leadership and value as a member of the organization. Following can be perceived as a minor role in organizational leadership.

Tensions arise when mentors are expected to give and followers are expected to take. Mentors can feel pressure from the responsibility to teach and guide, whereas followers can feel that they have a responsibility to learn and follow. Members of organizations are often selected or feel a need to play the role of mentor or follower which can discount the possibility of what embracing both roles may offer members and their organization. In the example, Gwen had established expectations for how her mentees should work and respond to her guidance. Gwen positioned herself as the leader/teacher and Maria was her student who required supervision and instruction from an experienced teacher. Maria "played the game" of follower, but internally she resisted the role of follower/mentee. Both Gwen and Maria were discounting to possibilities of reciprocal influence – albeit for different reasons.

It is possible to focus on building and sustaining reciprocal influence by nurturing organizational relationships where mentoring and following co-exist. How can we build reciprocal influence among individuals in an organization? How can we develop a culture of effective social support and organizational helpfulness? This chapter explores the possibilities that can emerge when organizations create a culture of & around mentoring and following.

Step 2: Find the Purpose of &: Reciprocal Influence

Mentoring & Following = Multiple Learners

If we recognize the limitations of one-way, give-or-take mentoring, why does it perpetuated? The answer can often be hat we teach as we were taught, we coach as we were coached, so we may slip into mentoring as we were mentored. Could it be that Gwen adopted her style of mentoring from her mentors? Poorly managed stress and anxiety can also cause people in positional power to over-control while people with less power can default to the status quo to avoid organizational conflicts. And, as we have discussed many times in this book, OR dynamics can be perpetuated simply because it's easier and less ambivalent. The result is a culture that enables partial learning instead of complete, reciprocal learning.

What does a more expansive view of mentoring look like? What does it mean to embrace reciprocal influence? The principle components of reciprocal influence assume a shift from a fixed mindset to a growth mindset. This shift involves openness, vulnerability, and the commitment to mutual growth, development, and advancement. Gwen provides an example of a fixed mindset when she uses her position to have Maria operate her way under the guise of mentoring. Even though Maria accepted and respected academia's cultural importance of mentoring, she tried at various times to be more open and communicative with Gwen to encourage greater flexibility. Could it have been the stress and anxiety of Gwen's job that led to greater rigidity in the pursuit of calm? And in that effort could Gwen have used mentoring as the rationale to justify her actions?

Bringing & into the process of mentoring starts to cultivate a mutual interest in the personal and professional development of both people, not just the follower. It's a bi-directional form of social support. This takes effort and requires skill, structure, and a commitment to building effective, authentic relationships that are values-centered. Be aware that shifting to this bi-directional form of support means that there are multiple learners in the equation now, not just one.

Small Shifts – Large Impact

As we look at various types of mentoring, we can explore how a small shift in perspective and commitment can lead to reciprocal influence. **Formal mentoring** programs, for example, are an attempt to create mentoring relationships through a matching-type process conducted by the organization. Single mentor-follower matches, while effective, can become too formal and hierarchical. As in the example, Gwen and Maria work in academia where formal mentors are assigned to protégées. In academia and other formal mentoring programs, mentors are thought to provide the necessary instruction to help the protégé follow the right path within the organization. Formal mentoring is often time-limited, focused on outcomes, transactional in nature, and intended to be emotionally passive. Intended is the operative word. Even the best mentoring programs struggle when individuals are "voluntold" to mentor or follow. But a slight shift in understanding social support and leading with values can honor the traditions of formal mentoring without sacrificing the developmental purpose of formal mentoring.

Johnson and Smith (2019) argue that instead of developing mentoring programs, organizations need "mentors of the moment" where all members of the organization seek opportunities in daily interactions to develop each other – mentoring and following. In fact, most individuals report that they prefer mentoring and following with a more reciprocal and mutual character – developing mentoring and following networks or constellations rather than 1-1 matches where you mentor or follow. This requires building and nurturing a value of positive micro-exchanges in the workplace to create informal mentoring and following experiences or "exposures" in the organization. Micro-exposures among mentors and followers assist individuals in becoming more aware of their current state, their desired state, and the gap that exists in between the two. The micro-exchanges then provide opportunity to formulate of action plans to decrease the gaps. (Richardson et al., 2021). Mentoring and following moments focus on taking advantage of daily opportunities to notice and engage one's colleagues. These mentoring and following exchanges bolster self-efficacy, commitment to the organization and create a context for the development and nurturing of transformational relationships. Richardson et al. (2021) maintain that this "micro" strategy works effectively with intergenerational mentoring and following. Specifically, developing a culture of mentors and followers of the moment provides a strategy for the management and transfer of thoughts and feelings necessary to create a more diverse, equitable, and inclusive environment.

These mentors of the moment are examples of **informal mentoring**, and for the most part, mentoring relationships are informal, developed through shared interests, admiration, or task demands. Informal mentoring tends to go beyond career-related issues to more in-depth personal sharing of interests, needs, and values (Noe, 1988). Most of the time, a younger, less experienced member of an organization will ask someone to mentor them on a particular issue. The mentors give of themselves to provide the help the mentees are desiring. While the relationship is typically a 1-1 ratio (one mentor with one follower), one can have multiple mentors for multiple issues. When authentic helpfulness becomes the primary purpose to informal mentoring, power and expertise become secondary and reciprocity is primary.

Upward mentoring or reverse mentoring, turns the traditional hierarchical approach to mentoring upside down. Rather than having a senior employee take a less experienced employee "under their wing," reverse mentoring places the more senior person as the primary learner or follower emphasizing the expertise of the junior person as the mentor (Murphy, 2012). The objective of reverse mentoring is primarily to enable leaders and senior managers to stay in touch with their organizations and the outside world. It is thought that advantages go both ways as more junior personnel have an opportunity to understand and be heard by more senior and experienced people. Organizations have reported positive results with reverse mentoring to enhance technological skills, diversity, equity, and inclusion of older or senior members of the organization. Following is fluid in reverse mentoring with reciprocal influence occurring across multiple issues. **Peer mentoring** is when the mentor is someone of equal standing, rank, or age (Kohler & Strain, 1990) of the protégé and has created a type of "formal-informal" mentorship that can demonstrate effectiveness in numerous contexts. Mentoring and following tends to flex depending upon the topics. With both upward mentoring and peer mentoring, the implied dynamics of deference and power are already disrupted to allow for more reciprocity and values expression.

Finally, there is **integrity mentoring**, or invisible mentoring (Frohmen & Howard, 2008). This is when someone's actions have an influence on others without intending to be influential. In our work on flourishing, we witnessed the powerful influence individuals can have when they live primarily with their values and manage fear and other difficult emotions in a healthy manner. People notice and respect such individuals and tend to emulate integrity, even if their values are different. More importantly, individuals who lead their lives with integrity tend to be interested in learning from others, resulting in reciprocal influence.

In essence, reciprocal influence results from the recognition that what is learned is not restricted to organizational experience or performance. When mentoring and following relationships are reciprocal, they can be inclusive of every aspect of life without being intrusive. Reciprocal influence can also create an empowering relationship for the follower and the mentor, and for the organization (Eagan, 1986). While numerous models exist that describe a stage-like progression from initiation to termination (Kram, 1983), the central theme appears to be movement toward a state of interdependency, working in concert with each other.

Step 3: Analyzing Your Team: Impact over Intent

Analyzing Organizational Helpfulness

No matter the type of mentoring relationship (e.g., formal, informal, micro-exposures, etc.), analyzing the impact of such relationships is important to determine whether the organization has developed a culture of helpfulness. The relational impact between mentor and follower is not universally positive, regardless of intent. As we see in the example, Maria had to spend time away from her work to appease Gwen's process demands. The impact of Gwen's style of mentoring resulted in Maria having to devote tremendous time and energy to emotional regulation, stress management, and continuously recommitting to not quitting amidst tremendous frustration. Think of how that energy could have been spent in more productive and effective ways. Mentors and followers must have an awareness of each other's bandwidth and receptivity. Mentors must also understand their followers and be attuned to when their mentoring approach is not effective. To build a culture of helpfulness and awareness, an organization should analyze the level of reciprocal influence in terms of helpfulness and social support.

Amabile, Fisher, and Pillemer (2014) asked employees to identify those in the organization that provided help and to rank the top five helpers. They were also asked to rate their #1 helper, their #5 helper, and a non-helper. These items assessed three characteristics of helping networks within the organization: competence, (how well the person did his or her job), trust (how comfortable the respondent was sharing thoughts and feelings with the person), and accessibility (how easily the respondent could obtain help from the person). The results demonstrated that trust and accessibility matter much more than competence when examining helping networks in organizations. Organizations work more effectively when members feel safe discussing problems and challenges with one another. Receiving help involved being vulnerable so it makes sense that people will turn to those they can trust with their thoughts and feelings. Accessibility involves being available, willing, and able to help. It should be noted that competence or expertise matters, but research has demonstrated that it matters less than trust and accessibility. These two characteristics of the helping network are influenced by how well an organization is explicit and clearly teaches how to seek, find, give, and receive help from others across the organization. An organization that clearly demonstrates helping as an expected behavior will enable everyone to be a part of the helping network. How might Gwen and Maria have answered such questions about their departmental culture?

Analyzing Social Support: From Omniscience to Active Curiosity

While leaders are often assigned the responsibility of mentoring in most organizations, years of experience, job titles, and power are no match to the social capital of those that provide social support needed in an organization. To develop a game plan for reciprocal influence, an analysis of the social support system operating in the organization is required. We suggest using a survey that measures different types of social support as suggested by Pines, Aronson, and Kafry (1981).

As a reminder from Chapter 4, social support has multiple dimensions beyond just emotional support (Hardy & Crace, 1993; Rosenfeld & Richman, 1997):

- *Listening* – Someone who actively listens without giving advice or being judgmental.
- *Emotional Support* – Someone you trust who provides comfort, care, and encouragement.
- *Emotional Challenge* – Someone who challenges you to examine your perspective, values, thoughts, and feelings.
- *Task Appreciation* – Someone who acknowledges your efforts and expresses appreciation for your work.
- *Task Challenge* – Someone who challenges the way you think about a task or activity that can lead to greater creativity, motivation, and involvement.
- *Reality Confirmation* – Someone who is coming from a similar reality or context and helps confirm your perspective of the world.
- *Tangible Assistance* – Someone who provides financial assistance, products, and/or gifts.
- *Personal Assistance* – Someone who provides services or help through the contribution of their time and energy.

At an individual level, it is important to develop a social support network because it is rare that any one individual can fulfill all dimensions of social support. When it comes to providing support, there are two vulnerabilities mentors need to be aware of: (1) Mentors may steer support toward the dimensions they feel most confident in providing, rather than being attuned to what a person is asking for. (2) Mentors may place pressure on themselves to predict and provide the exact type of support that is needed. Rather than demanding themselves to be all-knowingly omniscient, the most powerful form of support is leading with active curiosity and daring to ask the question, "How can I be of most support to you?" Mentors can have a greater impact by having the courage to be coached by the one seeking support. Aligning support-given with support-needed is the largest predictor of a team member believing they are in a culture of helpfulness. It's reasonable to assume that Maria did not find Gwen's support helpful because of Maria's wanted Listening, Emotional Support, and Task Appreciation, and Gwen was only giving Task Challenge.

Organizations that take the time to clarify dimensions of social support can create a culture that is resilient against turmoil and difficult emotional experiences. Organizations can assess their culture of helpfulness by assessing team members with the following questions and forming an aggregate of the results.

1. Who in the individual's environment is perceived to provide each type of social support? This can include team members, managers, friends, family, etc.
2. What is your current level of satisfaction in regards to each type of support received?
3. What are your expectations in obtaining higher levels of satisfaction for of each type of social support?
4. How important is each type of support for you at this time?

Examining the social support network of an organization as a whole provides an indication of (a) the extent to which members of an organization form an integrated support network, (b) whether some types of support are, in general, not being provided, and (c) whether some individuals are excluded from either giving or receiving social support from the organization. Assessing current satisfaction, expectations, and importance for each type of social support can provide valuable information in determining supportive aspects of an organization that need to be celebrated and/or need to be improved.

Organizations may assume that a culture of reciprocal influence based on helpfulness and social support is incompatible with individual responsibility and productivity. Indeed, many organizations have a long history of promoting competition among their members, therefore aiding a colleague could be seen as counterproductive to performance expectations. Margaret Heffernan however has provided evidence that a culture of helpfulness can lead to higher levels of organizational performance. She argues that helpfulness means you don't have to know everything; you just work with people who are good at getting and giving the help/support you need. This means that we need an organization that has a community of generous, honest, and resourceful people that nurture effective relationships (Heffernan 2015).

Step 4: Readying for &: Creating a Culture of Mutual Helpfulness and Support

The basic assumption of this chapter's essential & is that mentors and followers can learn and influence each other. Extending this principle to an organizational level indicates that a collection of learners can create an open culture of creativity, engagement, and support where the skills and abilities of individuals in the organization are amplified. Furthermore, reciprocal influence on the organizational level allows unsolvable challenges to be addressed and creative solutions to emerge. Wiseman and McKeown (2010) refer to this as the "Multiplier Effect." The mentor and follower, working in concert, multiply their energy by extracting and extending support to each other.

A year after Maria received her PhD, she was selected for a tenure-track position at a university across the country. Compared to the stresses of moving cross country or the challenges of a new position, Maria was most concerned with who would be her tenure advisor. The idea of being paired with someone like Gwen, her graduate school mentor, for seven years was terrifying. Luckily, Maria was paired with the Acting Department Chair, Lily. It was quickly evident why Lily was so well reputed in the department. During their first meeting, Lily asked questions Maria didn't expect. Questions like: What were Maria's specific research, publishing, and teaching goals? How could she best assist Maria for each area of focus? What resources and systems would best support Maria's work?

Through reciprocal influence, effective mentors can develop the leadership capacity of their followers, while increasing their own skills. They nurture the alignment between individual aspirations and organizational goals and values. Effective mentors have the power to create depth and loyalty within the organizations. Mentoring and following in organizations can motivate individuals to learn and grow by offering different and more challenging opportunities and providing support for further learning and growth. Effective mentoring and following can also helpful recruiting; retaining talent; and enhancing commitment among employees. The following are some practical strategies to build organizational culture toward mutual helpfulness and support.

Setting the Stage for Reciprocal Influence

Offer mentoring and following training/opportunities. Don't assume that individuals are clear about their role in giving and taking from others, or that individuals know how to mentor and follow. Effective communication and building trust are the two foundational skills of this training. If individuals are "expected" to mentor and follow, such expectations should be explicit and transparent. In addition, to enhance commitment to developing a mentoring and following culture, consideration should be given to creating a reward structure that reinforces effective mentoring and following within the organization.

Give agency to the team member for setting mentoring and following goals and objectives. While organizational goals and objectives are important components of mentoring and following, it is important to provide the space for mentors and followers to set goals and objectives that they will pursue together. Providing participants with control over this aspect of the process encourages belief and commitment to the building an effective relationship. It is important to make sure that goals are both realistic and measurable.

Grow and develop a mentoring and following culture. Nurture development by inquiring and assessing the effectiveness of your mentoring and following culture. Stay on top of organizational health, social support networks, and organizational trust. Use data collected from the analysis in Step 3 to foster deeper discussions around these issues. Demonstrate value for mentoring that both gives and receives support every day. Reciprocal mentoring and following culture should prioritize mutual learning, trust, and care at its core, as opposed to a hierarchical matching program.

Actively attend to diversity, equity, inclusion, and justice issues. Take the time and effort to understand the system-level barriers that marginalized individuals in the organization have to manage. Explore what practices, procedures, or behaviors might be seen as supportive or dismissive. Moreover, examine what practices are in place that can discourage talented members from feeling included and valued in the organization. Use values as a foundational reference to have conversations about power, privilege, and marginalization. For example, a rich and robust discussion can occur from the following values-centered questions:

- What personal values do you feel are affirmed in your work culture and what values are difficult to act on in the way you would prefer?
- Outside of work, where do you have the ability to act on your values and where do your values feel marginalized?

- How do you experience privilege and where do you experience marginalization?
- What forms of social support, impact mentoring, and following that would currently be most helpful for you in managing these areas?

Mentoring and following is a network of relationships. Rather than think of mentoring and following as 1-1, life-long, or one size fits all relationship, it can be more beneficial to view mentoring and following as a network system with individuals moving in an out of different networks to give and receive the support needed to flourish.

Mentoring and following is a dynamic process. Understand that mentoring and following is a dynamic rather than static process impacted by environmental influences. What was effective mentoring and following for one time-period or team may not be effective for another. Changes in culture and/or environment will impact how a mentoring and following structure can thrive.

Mindset for Managing Conflict in the Mentoring Relationship

It is inevitable that as diverse perspectives are embraced and open expression is valued, conflict and tensions may arise. How can mentors and followers find meaningful opportunities to grow and learn through conflict, rather than slipping into power dynamics and competitiveness? The following are mindset tips to healthfully step into conflict:

Don't Try to Help, Focus on Learning – Active curiosity, not expertise, is the number one predictor of successful support and conflict management. Define success by engagement in the process rather than defining success by outcomes. Seek to understand before being understood.

Align Support Given with Support Sought – Discern the type of social support that one is seeking and try to match that. "How can I best support you right now?"

Apply Reasonable Person Theory – Are reactions congruent with the situation? What might be adding to the intensity?

Honor the Reactions, Challenge the Conclusions – Validate others' reactions to a situation and challenge any premature conclusions they may be making out of fear or hurt.

Find Values in the Weeds – Stay actively curious to find the core "why" and values that are being triggered in the conflict.

Honor and Manage Your Own Filters – Be aware of how our values can influence the way we view a situation and how we deal with conflict.

Replace "But" with "And," avoid "Why" – Keep your language as inclusive as possible. Words such as "but" and "why" can often have a different impact than intended. "But" can negate the value of the first half of a sentence (e.g., "Nice job but next time I want you to be more concise in your answers"). "Why" is often received as judgment (e.g., Why did you take that approach in your report?").

Stalling as an Effective Strategy – If possible, it can be beneficial to wait and meet when conflicting parties can be fully engaged and mindful.

Manage Chronic Storms with Structure and Support – Accept that for some the same conversation and rules may need to be revisited repeatedly for healthy change to occur.

"What else is true?" – When possible, expand on the broader realities present in the organization and among the individuals in conflict. The point of this tactic is to identify 'What else is true?' in order to break from the narrow tunnel vision of the conflict.

Whatever shape a mentoring and following program may take in an organization, remember that mentoring and following is an intentional process. It can change a culture from falling into the natural tendency to mentor Or follow to a culture that embraces the strength of openness and learning and connects that strength to greater organizational productivity and effectiveness. The *cultural humility* of reciprocal influence can be a powerful portal to dealing with the many challenges of organizational flourishing.

Step 5: Giving Voice to &: The Power of Cultural Humility

In a few years, Maria received tenure at her university. Lily had largely been a hands-off mentor, checking in regularly to see if Maria needed any resources or a listening ear. Maria flourished like she hadn't in grad school. Being able to freely explore her research and teaching load without being micromanaged allowed Maria to develop pedagogical techniques and research insights that began to earn her acclaim in the field.

Several semesters into her tenure, Maria was assigned to advise a new tenure-track hire. She felt enthusiastically ready to mentor someone. After her terrible experience with Gwen followed by such a positive experience with Lily as an advisor, Maria knew how to be the best mentor a new hire could ask for.

Spencer needed guidance. Point him in a direction; show him how to do something; provide basic instruction, and Spencer dutifully went at tasks headlong. He would eventually personalize his approach, but needed an initial foundation to have confidence when tackling new endeavors. Open-ended direction that forced him to improvise was overwhelming. He often found himself over-thinking or doubtful to the point of being unable to start. His whole life Spencer had heard the more he was challenged to improvise, the better off he'd be. But Spencer didn't find that to be true, the anxiety was always overwhelming, and the work regularly suffered. When he had a little bit of direction, something to work off of, he tended to fall into projects with interest and tenacity. His tenure-advisor, Maria, clearly believed in the sink-or-swim approach. Aside from her weekly check-ins, she seemed to stay away from Spencer. During the weekly check-ins, Spencer tried vocalizing all the questions he had collected over the week, but Maria always answered with vague ideas, "How do you feel your rubrics should be adjusted?"

"I don't know. What have you done in the past?"

"My approach isn't important. It's about you having the freedom to develop in your own way."

Initially, Spencer had been excited about working with Maria. She was rapidly garnering a name for herself in the field, but the clutter of her office, her broad advice, and the lack of direct instruction was wreaking havoc on Spencer's anxiety. He started looking to others for concrete advice: The other tenure-track hire became someone Spencer could vent to. Another professor in the department became someone Spencer could get quick, direct answers from. Spencer even found helpful mentor-moments with the department head, Lily, who gave encouraging but challenging feedback that was clear and useful. Spencer started to rely on Lily's input to the point where Lily finally asked, "Spencer, are you bringing these questions to Maria?"

Spencer hesitated not wanting to speak ill of his advisor, "Yes. . . of course. Maria's great, but. . . I like your feedback as well."

Lily sensed the issue, "Have you told Maria what kind of feedback and advice you're looking for?"

"I probably could be better about that." Spencer replied knowing he had been clear about the advice he preferred.

Spencer was worried when Lily scheduled a group meeting between him, Maria, and Lily. He started to preemptively apologize to Maria, but Lily began, "Spencer and Maria, I want to create a supervised forum so that both of you can share how the advising relationship is progressing."

Maria was surprised. She thought she'd been a great mentor to Spencer. She recalled flashes of Gwen's boot camp style of mentorship. She never did anything like that to Spencer. "I thought it was going well. Spencer's work is developing at a pace that can absolutely lead to tenure."

Spencer responded quickly, "Thank you, Maria. It is going well. I don't want you to think that I'm going behind your back or anything. I was just getting feedback from different people."

"I want you to be direct, Spencer." Lily interrupted, "This is the time to be clear. How can Maria be the mentor you need her to be?"

If he wasn't clear and direct now, then there would be little chance the advising relationship would change. Spencer faced Maria, "This may make me sound weak, but I don't like being thrown into the deep end. I don't do well with the hands-off approach because I end up spending too much time trying to get started. I appreciate you trying to strengthen my creative, improvising skills, but I could really benefit from some concrete examples. When I have some guidance, I don't get hung up on starting. I just fall into the work."

Maria recalled Gwen's micromanaging demands preventing her from 'falling into her work,' and now Maria's intention to give Spencer space had had the same outcome — the exact effect she wanted to avoid.

Lily interjected, "Maria, you taught me so much when I was your advisor. I used to keep a watchful eye on advisees and provide ample methodologies for them to try out. I had a lot of success with that approach. But when you started here, you made it very clear that you needed space to flourish. It was difficult for me to give you that space. I felt like I was failing you. And when I did give you concrete advice, it tended to have a stifling effect. It took some time to learn how to give you open-ended feedback that inspired your creativity."

"You were a great mentor." Maria responded.

"I wasn't so great at the beginning. It took time for me to get used to the style you needed, but I learned so much from our advising relationship. It taught me how to improvise and manage ambivalence in my own work."

Maria turned to Spencer explaining, "I had a brutal advisor in grad school. It was like boot camp. And then Lily was such a great mentor to me. I promised myself I'd never be anything like my grad school advisor. I wanted to be like Lily."

"You can be more like me by trying to learn from what Spencer needs." Lily said and then turned to Spencer, "And Spencer, you can learn, as I did, from Maria's approach. She is providing you with opportunities to be creative. Don't be too quick to shut down her approach." Turning back to Maria, "And I'm sure Maria will make more of an effort to give you guidance and concrete direction."

Spencer enthusiastically turned to Maria, "I'm a huge admirer of your career. I want to know how you do things. I'm dying to try out your procedures."

"That you can work off of and make your own," Maria added.

"Exactly."

"I can adjust to that."

References

Amabile, T.M., Fisher, C.M., & Pillemer, J. (2014). IDEO's Culture of Helping. *Harvard Business Review*, 3–9.

Eagan, J.B. (1986). Characteristics of mentor teachers' mentor-protégé relationships. In W.A. Gray & M.M. Gray (Eds.), *Mentoring: Aid to excellence in education, the family and the community*. International Association for Mentoring.

Frohmen, D., & Howard, R. (2008). *Leadership the hard way. Why can't leadership be taught and how you can learn it anyway*. Jossey-Bass.

Hardy, C.J., & Crace, R.K. (1993). The dimensions of social support when dealing with sport injuries. In D. Pargman (Ed.), *Psychological basis of sport injuries* (pp. 121–144). Fitness Information Technology, Inc.

Heffernan, M. (2015). *The secret ingredient that makes some teams better than others*. https://ideas.ted.com/the-secret-ingredient-that-makes-some-teams-better-than-others/

Johnson, B., & Smith, D.G. (2019, December 30). Real mentorship starts with company culture, not formal programs. *Harvard Business Review*. https://hbr.org/2019/12/real-mentorship-starts-with-company-culture-not-formal-programs

Kohler, F.W., & Strain, P.S. (1990). Peer-assisted interventions: Early promises, notable acheivements, and future aspirations. *Clinical Psychology Review, 10*, 441–452.

Kram, K.E. (1983). Phases of the mentor relationship. *Academy of Management Journal, 26*(4), 608–626.

Murphy, W.M. (2012). Reverse mentoring at work: Fostering cross-generational learning and developing millennial leaders. *Human Resource Management, 51*(4), 549–574.

Noe, R.A. (1988). An investigation of the determinants of successful assigned mentoring relationships. *Personnel Psychology, 41*, 457–479.

Pines, A.M., Aronson, E., & Kafry, D. (1981). *Burnout*. Free Press.

Richardson, E., Newsham, T.M.K., Gordaon, J., Oetjen, R., Fisher, D., Schroeder, L.H., et al. (2021). Intergenerational micro-mentoring: Addressing ageism and inclusion in the workplace. *The Chronicle of Mentoring and Coaching, 5*(Special Issue 14), 39–44.

Rosenfeld, L.B., & Richman, J.M. (1977). Developing effective social support: Team building and the social support process. *Journal of Applied Sport Psychology, 9*, 133–153.

Wiseman, L., & McKeown, G. (2010). *Multiplier: How the best leaders make everyone smarter*. HarperCollins Publisher.

10

IN CLOSING

TRANSFORMATIVE OPTIMIZER: YOU

As Chief Wellness Officer, Marra invested her creativity, talent, and hard work into shaping the culture of her company to embrace both stress & wellness. It was not a linear process and wasn't without its share of disappointments. However, even with all the detours, it was starting to become evident in who they recruited and retained that the company was moving in the right direction. Professionals were attracted to the company because of their emphasis on wellness, sustained productivity, and increased value in their industry. Some employees had left and it was mainly the people who relied on the Or of stress glorification culture.

The company had moved beyond rhetoric and platitudes. They were living an & culture with integrity. The C Suite had seen the impact of Marra's work on the overall vitality of the organization. Marra had gained quite a reputation in the field and in her city. After a keynote speech at a Chamber of Commerce luncheon, a local company asked her to do some consulting so they could explore more wellness strategies.

After a morning with their leadership team, the CEO raised her hand and said, "I'm a bottom line person. This all sounds good and you obviously

DOI: 10.4324/9781003265726-10

have the success to demonstrate that your approach is effective. It also sounds like it's going to require a significant investment of time and energy on our part. But before we take this on, I'm curious if you could distill the most valuable components of this work down to the key takeaways. If you had to explain your success in a couple of minutes, what would you say?"

Marra thought for a minute. Her mind drifted back to her dinner with Stacey two years ago when she was quite concerned about the new position. What had worked over the years to get from that place of concern to this place of success? She had been so entrenched in this ambiguous and ambivalent work that she hadn't taken the time to distill it to its essence. Marra replied, "What a great question," the go-to response that allowed for more time to think. Then she remembered an exercise she had taken the group through in the first six months that had gained traction with the team. They had constantly referred back to it in the months since. "First, and foremost, this work doesn't lend itself to distillation. That's kind of the point — to respect the complexity of the people and relationships of each team. But your question is a fair one.

"If I had to break it down as to what I thought was most effective for our group, it would be our committed mindsets. Throughout our work, I found that there were times when we needed to focus or refocus on a particular perspective or mindsets, as we referred to them. Over the past two years, we learned a lot about strategies and we learned a lot about ourselves as a collective. When things would drift, we would return to a mindset, or focus point, that was most relevant. There were ten that came up most frequently for us, to the point where we all had a list of them displayed in our office. At our staff meetings, we would remind ourselves of them so they were in the forefront of our minds."

Honor our humanity. It was important to understand but not judge why we would drift into Or thinking.

Insight is necessary but insufficient for change. Practicing the work was critical.

Values must lead. This work is hard and nonlinear, so everyone had to see the why behind the work. Values have to lead; otherwise, fear-based need and power creep in.

If it ain't scary, it ain't important. There's a dynamic relationship between values and fear. It helped to remind ourselves that everything we care about has uncertainty attached to it. The goal is not to conquer fear and stress but to develop confidence in managing them.

Breadth equals depth. Diversity of thought, experiences, and values are the best predictors of organizational flourishing, but that inevitably would bring tensions.

Horizontal values over vertical values. It was easy to slip into the temptation of always following the values of the positional leaders. Everyone's values mattered and we constantly reminded ourselves of the "Team Values" that we had assessed from the aggregate of all of our individual values, including but not limited to the leaders.

Embrace the Improv Mindset. In Improv, everyone commits to "Yes, and." There is never a "no" or a "but" or an "or."

It's hard, and it's only hard. We continuously reminded ourselves that this hard work is not beyond us.

Seek to understand first, be understood second. When managing conflict, we committed to stay curious with each other instead of conclusive.

Choose deliberate compassion. At times, the stress and absurdity of the world around our work caused us not to be our best selves where we would unintentionally step on sensitivities. We committed to seeing first the value that everyone brings and second the challenges they bring. We also committed to leading with the values we bring and taking responsibility for managing our own challenges. We didn't wait until we felt kind, forgiving, or respectful. We chose them because of the rightness of them.

"So honestly, I don't know if these factors that made a difference for us will have the same impact on your company, but with time and curiosity you can learn the ones that matter most to your company." The CEO smiled and said, "You're the first consultant I've ever met who has said, 'I don't know.'..."

"I don't know & I do."

We are grateful for your curiosity and tenacity in staying with principles of the book. They can often feel ambiguous and counter to our natural inclination. We are admiring of those who have or are ready to courageously step into this work. You, & your values, & your effort, & your healthy perspective are enough to have transformational impact on &. While we have focused on eight essential &s, there are no doubt many other &s that organizations manage. We encourage you to consider the framework presented in this book as you build your "& bank" and to share your wisdom with us. Please consider us a support and your biggest fans.

APPENDIX 1

OVERVIEW OF GIVING VOICE TO VALUES AND AUTHENTIC EXCELLENCE

Giving Voice to Values

(adapted from *"Giving Voice to Values: How to Speak Your Mind When You Know What's Right"*; Gentile, 2010)

Giving Voice to Values (GVV) is a practice-based approach developed by Mary Gentile to enact one's values through situational practice scenarios. With practice, a moral muscle is built so that one's voice and actions are more likely to enact one's values in the context of a specific scenario. Action is practiced by the development of scripts that allow for the voicing of values in the workplace. While it is often said that practice makes perfect, GVV has demonstrated that practice makes permanent. The central question is "If I were to act on my values in this situation, what would I say and/or do?" GVV is a practice-based pedagogy that focuses on enhancing one's competence and confidence in acting on their values. GVV is grounded upon what is called the "Thought Experiment" where the question is not, 'What is the right thing to do?' the question is, 'How do we get the right thing done?' The key to this approach is deciding on what to say to whom and how. The issue is not deciding what to do, rather it is on how to give voice to one's values. Scripting and practice are essential to effectively giving voice to values. When we develop the skills to take the action away from right and wrong into the realm of practice, we align our actions with our values and build our moral muscle.

To give voice does not imply some cathartic process of sounding off about one's ideals or engaging in a self-righteous rant. Giving Voice to Values refers to several forms of expression, for example, data gathering, coalition building, finding allies, identification of stakeholders, exploring purposes, crafting responses, and even choosing to be silent when appropriate.

Some people find ways to voice and act on their values and other do not. While there is a laundry list of strategies that one can adopt, the pivotal moment occurs when one decides to speak – giving voice to their values. Once the decision to speak is made, the next step determining how to speak. Either/Or thinking leads us down a path of either standing up and declaring our position Or we can remain silent. This either/Or framing of options can lead to great silence and/or an ineffective voice.

GVV begins with the assumption that most of us want to bring our whole selves to work—skills, ambitions, and values. Yet, we know from experience and research that most of us will encounter values conflicts in our careers – when the way we want to live and the things we want to accomplish seem in conflict with the expectations of the organizations we work for.

The conviction behind GVV – one that is supported by both research as well as practice – is that "practice makes permanent." We tend to develop habitual behaviors around our actions; and decisions and while there are many different ways we can express our values, the situation and the audience are two critical considerations. In addition, the organizational culture strongly impacts the ability to voice our values. Increasing our confidence and competence through pre-scripting, practice, and coaching prepares us to be effective in voicing our values.

Giving Voice to Values is designed to help individuals learn to recognize, clarify, and act on their values – particularly when conflicts arise. The distinctive features of the Giving Voice to Values Curriculum include:

1. A focus on effective strategies to voice ones values.
2. An emphasis on the importance of finding an alignment between one's individual sense of purpose and that of the organization.

3. The opportunity to develop and practice responses to the most frequently heard reasons and rationalizations for *not* acting on one's values.
4. The opportunity to provide peer feedback and coaching to enhance effectiveness.

It's also important to understand that since there are so many different ways to voice our values, we can look for the approach that not only seems most likely to be effective in our particular situation, but also the one that is most comfortable given our own personal style and communication strengths. Through pre-scripting, practice, and coaching we can increase the likelihood that we will actually voice our values.

Often, a situational conflict contains an ethical component which can lead to Either/Or responses where we can act as Either saints Or martyrs. However, we can actually better address ethical conflicts by being competent, skillful, and prepared. It is important to consider the needs, desires, and emotional investments of the individuals to whom we are speaking instead of focusing exclusively on our own interests. Re-framing "voice" as "dialogue" – which includes listening – is another important quality of giving voice to our values.

In order to develop the ability to express our values we need to address the following questions:

•   What are the main arguments you are trying to counter? What are the *reasons and rationalizations* you need to address?
•   What's at *stake* for the key parties including those who disagree with you? What's at *stake* for you?
•   What *levers* can you use to influence those who disagree with you?
•   What is your most *powerful and persuasive response* to the reasons and rationalizations you need to address? To whom should the argument be made? When and in what context?

GVV invites us to engage in the "Thought Experiment" by answering: "What if you were going to act on this values-based position? How could you be effective?"

Building Your Moral Muscle Memory. The foundation of the GVV pedagogy is based upon the following three questions: (1) What's at stake? (2) What are the reasons and rationalizations that need to be addressed? and (3) What levers can be used to influence those who disagree with your position? Collectively, the answers to these questions constitute the basis of the script for constructing a persuasive argument for effecting values-based change and action planning. This approach is based on the idea that scripting and rehearsal lead to values-based action. Scripting, practicing, and building your "moral muscle memory" can help one speak up when values conflicts emerge.

The following pillars give structure to the GVV action-oriented practices and teaching methods.

1. **Values:** GVV employs the language of values to engage with people's deepest motivation and goals. A relatively short list of widely shared (common) values: e.g. honesty, respect, responsibility, fairness, and compassion provide the foundation for ethical conversations across cultural, organizational, and/or situational boundaries.
2. **Choice:** GVV is about implementing one's values. This pillar emphasizes an individual's choice to act or not act on their values. Knowing the factors that support action or inaction leads to an understanding that choice is always present and it is possible to appeal to that capacity for choice in others.
3. **Normality:** Values are present in all our decisions and influence normal aspects of everyday life. Values conflicts and opportunities are to be an expected aspect of every role and life situation. This leads to the assumption that responses and actions can be prepared and scripted to reduce the risk of shock, over-reaction, or hasty decision-making when addressing conflicts and opportunities.
4. **Purpose:** Acknowledging and reflecting on one's personal and professional purpose can be a source of strength and guidance when values conflicts emerge. A broad sense of purpose also allows a greater awareness of the responsibilities that accompany professional work and helps to build connections with others' sense of purpose.
5. **Self-knowledge, Self-image, and Alignment:** Responding to values conflicts requires self-knowledge – an understanding of one's strengths and preferred styles of interaction and communication. Having a "self-story" that is values based supports actions that are consistent with who one desires to be now and in the future.
6. **Voice:** The pillar of voice recognizes that the opportunity to express and act on one's values should be a fundamental aspect of all organizations.

Practicing and engaging in values-based conversations is essential for the development of flourishing organizations.

7. **Rationalizations:** Justifications for not acting on our values can always be found. These rationalizations silence the expression of core values and function as disablers. Identifying these disablers and developing responses to counter them is at the heart of GVV.

Each of the above pillars provides the basis for learning to effectively give voice to our values. These pillars provide a structure for effectively addressing values-conflicts through the application of the GVV process.

Each of our chapters was framed around a GVV process to personalize and internalize the work of creating flourishing "&" cultures. It is adapted from the following GVV process designed to script, practice, and build muscle-memory around giving voice to our values with others.

1. **The Ethical Issue** – What is wrong? What are the possibilities for dealing with what is perceived as wrong? "How will I respond to this issue?" The key to this step is acknowledging that there is a values conflict.

2. **Purpose and Choice** – Reflection about one's personal and professional purpose? "What is my purpose in voicing my values in this situation? What is my Why? What are my choices?"

3. **Process and Data / Stakeholder Analysis** – "What is at stake for others and how do I engage them? Who are my allies and/or key stakeholders?"

4. **Scripting and Acting / Crafting a Powerful Response** – What are potential arguments? "What will I say and do? What are my options? Who are my allies?" Is there any research to do? This step is design to develop and practice effective GVV scripts and to identify rationalizations, levers, and enablers that facilitate achieving one's purpose. "What does my Game Plan entail and who can I count on for support?"

5. **Scripting and Coaching** –Scripting and practicing enabling conversations with peer coaches. "What will I say or do?"

Authentic Excellence Initiative

(adapted from "Authentic Excellence: Flourishing and Resilience in a Relentless World"; Crace & Crace, 2020)

Authentic Excellence reflects a redefinition of excellence based on one's sense of purpose and healthy values management. Success is seen as the courage to act on one's values and the basis of motivation and decision making is shifted from being fear-centered to values-centered. This shift results in a deeper level of productivity, fulfillment, and resilience.

Values are defined as the basic set of beliefs that guide our motivation, decision making, and behavior. Values also serve as the lens for how we evaluate ourselves and others. The *Authentic Excellence Initiative* helps individuals and groups develop deeper relationships with their values and to build effective coping skills to manage the noise of a comparative and competitive world. Flourishing is the result of intentionality toward three primary factors: authenticity, integrity, and resilience. It is not enough to know our values – values clarification. We must also develop this clarification into an ever-changing, relational understanding of our values. How do we manage our individual values relationships? How might we deal with the nuances and complexities of how our values interact with our lives? And how are our values affecting how we interact with each other. By developing deeper relationships with our values, we are more likely to act on them as well as cope when the world prevents us from acting on them. When we align our behavior with our values, we increase the probability of living with purpose rather than living at our neurology – patterned responses based upon fear and comfort.

Authentic Excellence's 5 Paradigm Shifts

The *Authentic Excellence Initiative* centers five linear paradigm shifts to train toward a deeper level of effectiveness that includes more consistent productivity, fulfillment, and resilience:

1. **Shifting from values clarification to values relationship.** We must go beyond knowing what our values are to a level of interaction with our values that is relational. That interaction involves understanding how our values are alive in our daily functioning; how they manifest in our

decision-making and actions; how they interact with each other; and how they cause us fulfillment and stress. *How do we develop a healthy relationship with our values?*

2. **Shifting from experience-minded to integrity minded.** We can define our worth by whether we are getting a fair return on our investment of time and energy. However, one of the cornerstones of confidence and a healthy self-esteem is a personal sense of integrity – how well our behavior aligns with our values. To flourish, we must shift from defining our successes and work as a collection of outcomes in the form of equity to defining success and work by the degree our daily behavior reflects our values. *What do our values look like in action and how do we distinguish healthy from unhealthy expression of our values?*

3. **Shifting from reducing fear through over-control and avoidance to holding fear well.** Fear-based excellence compels us to manage fear through over-control or avoidance. People who consistently flourish are not less afraid, they just hold fear well. They understand that because of uncertainty, fear will always accompany what is important to them. Their objective is to keep fear in perspective so that their values primarily lead their behavior rather than fear. *How do we learn how to hold fear well so we can act on our values?*

4. **Shifting from avoidance of difficult emotions to confidence in managing difficult emotions.** We can be highly productive, fulfilled, and resilient yet still experience difficult emotions like hurt, anger, worry, and guilt. How do we thrive through disappointment or heartbreak? When we flourish, we are less concerned about avoiding difficult emotions like hurt, and are more focused on managing hurt in a healthy manner. *How do we develop confidence in managing difficult emotions?*

5. **Shifting from a chronically evaluate mindset to an expressive mindset.** To flourish, we must shift from constant self-evaluation to a mindset where we are defining our success by the expression of our values. Interestingly, an expressive mindset is the same mindset that promotes the flow or zone state optimal performance. *How do we develop a values-based expressive mindset?*

APPENDIX 2

LIFE VALUES INVENTORY
PRINT COPY

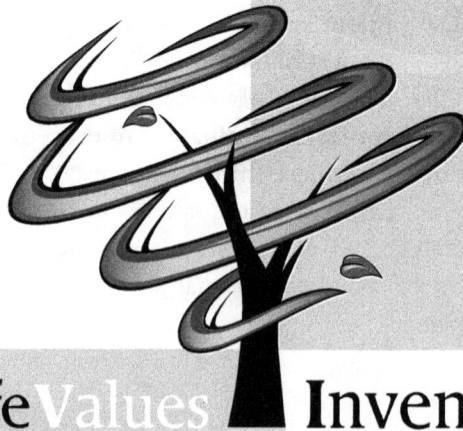

Life**Values** Inventory
CLARIFYING YOUR PERSONAL TRUTH

R. Kelly Crace, Ph.D. & Duane Brown, Ph.D.

Life Values ❦ Inventory
CLARIFYING   YOUR   PERSONAL   TRUTH

Developed by:

R. Kelly Crace, Ph.D. & Duane Brown, Ph.D.

Applied Psychology Resources, Inc.
Psychological Consulting, Counseling and Educational Resoces

For more information on how to use your values for personal development
please visit www.lifevaluesinventory.org

Instructions

Values are beliefs that influence people's behavior and decision making. For example, if people believe that telling the truth is very important, they will try to be truthful when they deal with other people. Research has shown that understanding our values is one of the most important factors in determining satisfaction in our work, relationships, and leisure activities. All healthy personal values have a social context and, therefore, a certain level of societal "should" or moral weight associated with them. The reason for our focus on personal values has to do with the process of clarifying one's authenticity through a values lens. We believe if a person can accurately assess what truly matters to them at various times in their life and discern how those values can be healthfully expressed and managed in their behavior, then they are more equipped to understand and manage the relationship between their personal values and societally-weighted moral values. The Life Values Inventory is designed to help you clarify and prioritize your values and serve as a blueprint for future decision making.

On the following pages is a list of beliefs that guides people's behavior and helps them make important decisions. Read each one and then choose the response (1-5) that best describes how often the belief guides your behavior. Before you begin, complete the following practice item by circling the number that best describes how this belief guides your behavior now.

	...GUIDES MY BEHAVIOR:			
	Seldom	Sometimes	Frequently	
Being Healthy	1	2	3	4	5

If a belief in being healthy seldom guides your behavior, circle 1. If being healthy frequently guides your behavior, circle 5. If the best answer for you is between 1 and 5, circle the number (2, 3, or 4) that most accurately describes how this belief guides your behavior.

Read each item carefully and circle only one response. Usually your first idea is the best indicator of how you feel. Answer every item. There are no right or wrong answers. Your choices should describe your own values, not the values of others.

Important tips:

(1) All of the items reflect positive values. Avoid rating all items as 4 or 5. Use your behavior as a guide to your ratings.

(2) When thinking about your current behavior, think in terms of this general time in your life, not in terms of today or this past week.

Values Items

Add up your ratings for each three-item grouping and write the sum in the "Score" column. The letters (A, B, C, etc.) correlate to each of the **14 life values**, which will make up your "Values Profile" on the following page.

Example:

2+3+4

Challenging myself to achieve	1	2	③	4	5		
Improving my performance	1	2	3	④	5	→ ⊕ 9	A
Working hard to do better	1	②	3	4	5		

Page 4 ➤ Values Profile ➤ A ➤ Achievement *(Score)* ➤ 9

	...GUIDES MY BEHAVIOR:						
	Seldom	Sometimes	Frequently			Score	
Challenging myself to achieve	1	2	3	4	5	⊕	A
Improving my performance	1	2	3	4	5		
Working hard to do better	1	2	3	4	5		
Being liked by others	1	2	3	4	5	⊕	B
Being accepted by others	1	2	3	4	5		
Feeling as though I belong	1	2	3	4	5		
Protecting the environment	1	2	3	4	5	⊕	C
Preserving nature	1	2	3	4	5		
Appreciating the beauty of nature	1	2	3	4	5		
Being sensitive to others' needs	1	2	3	4	5	⊕	D
Helping others	1	2	3	4	5		
Being concerned about the rights of others	1	2	3	4	5		
Coming up with new ideas	1	2	3	4	5	⊕	E
Being creative	1	2	3	4	5		
Discovering new things or ideas	1	2	3	4	5		
Having financial success	1	2	3	4	5	⊕	F
Making money	1	2	3	4	5		
Being wealthy	1	2	3	4	5		
Taking care of my body	1	2	3	4	5	⊕	G
Being in good physical shape	1	2	3	4	5		
Being athletic	1	2	3	4	5		

Values Items
(Continued)

	...GUIDES MY BEHAVIOR:					Score	
	Seldom	Sometimes	Frequently				
Downplaying compliments or praise	1	2	3	4	5		
Being quiet about my successes	1	2	3	4	5		H
Avoiding credit for my accomplishments	1	2	3	4	5		
Being independent	1	2	3	4	5		
Giving my opinion	1	2	3	4	5		I
Having control over my time	1	2	3	4	5		
Accepting my place in my family or group	1	2	3	4	5		
Respecting the traditions of my family or group	1	2	3	4	5		J
Making decisions with my family or group in mind	1	2	3	4	5		
Relying on objective facts	1	2	3	4	5		
Relying on logic to solve problems	1	2	3	4	5		K
Being analytical	1	2	3	4	5		
Having time to myself	1	2	3	4	5		
Having quiet time to think	1	2	3	4	5		L
Having a private place to go	1	2	3	4	5		
Being reliable	1	2	3	4	5		
Being trustworthy	1	2	3	4	5		M
Meeting my obligations	1	2	3	4	5		
Believing in a higher power	1	2	3	4	5		
Believing there is something greater than ourselves	1	2	3	4	5		N
Living in harmony with my spiritual beliefs	1	2	3	4	5		

Values Profile

Scores		Rankings

A. _____   **ACHIEVEMENT**   _____
It is important to challenge myself and to work hard to improve.

B. _____   **BELONGING**   _____
It is important to be accepted by others and to feel included.

C. _____   **CONCERN FOR THE ENVIRONMENT**   _____
It is important to protect and preserve the environment.

D. _____   **CONCERN FOR OTHERS**   _____
The wellbeing of others and helping others are important.

E. _____   **CREATIVITY**   _____
It is important to have new ideas, create new things, or be creatively expressive.

F. _____   **FINANCIAL PROSPERITY**   _____
It is important to be financially successful.

G. _____   **HEALTH AND ACTIVITY**   _____
It is important to be healthy and physically active.

H. _____   **HUMILITY**   _____
It is important to be humble and modest about my accomplishments.

I. _____   **INDEPENDENCE**   _____
It is important to have a sense of autonomy with my decisions and actions.

J. _____   **INTERDEPENDENCE**   _____
The expectations of my family, social group, team or organization are important.

K. _____   **OBJECTIVE ANALYSIS**   _____
It is important to use logical principles to understand and solve problems.

L. _____   **PRIVACY**   _____
It is important to have time alone.

M. _____   **RESPONSIBILITY**   _____
It is important to be dependable and trustworthy.

N. _____   **SPIRITUALITY**   _____
It is important to have spiritual beliefs that reflect being a part of something greater than myself.

RANKINGS. You have completed the first step of values clarification by rating individual items on pages 2 & 3. The second step is to rank the 14 life values scales. Use your scores listed above as a guide to rank the values that are most important and influence your behavior. Begin the process by identifying your most important life value that frequently guides your behavior and place a "1" in the right column labeled "Rankings" by that value. Then identify your second most important value, your third, and so forth. At the end of this process, you should have assigned all of the values listed above a number ranging from 1-14. You may find it difficult to rank a few values because of tied scores or because they are so close in importance. In this instances, use your current behavior as a guide to let you know what values are currently the most influential.

Preferred Values Expression

Aligning Behavior with Desired Values

As you review the values profile of your current behavior, you may want to make a few adjustments in how you devote your time and energy. Look carefully at your values rankings on page 4. Thinking of the next six months to a year, what changes in your behavior would you like to make? Be realistic in your adjustments. Remember that you only have so many hours in a day and that your current environment may impact how much you can adjust your devotion of time and energy.

The four categories below each represent a different relationship between the importance you place on a value and how much attention (time and energy) you devote to it.

Looking at your values rankings on page 4, select the category that *best* fits each value.

High Priority	Over-Attention	Under-Attention	Low Priority
Values in this category are important to me AND I frequently act on them.	I am focusing on these values more than I would prefer.	I am not focusing on these values as much as I would prefer.	These values are less important and I don't act on them very frequently.

Preferred Values Expression

Where you Express your Values:
Values & Life Roles

We express our values through our life roles. Since it is rare that one life role, such as work, satisfies all of our values, we often devote time and energy to several roles. While we may be involved in many activities and relationships, most people divide their time into three major life roles: (1) Work/Academics; (2) Important Relationships; and (3) Leisure/Community Activities. **Using the values on page 4, list the values you hope to have satisfied in each of these three life roles.**

You can list a value in more than one role. If there is another important role that doesn't fit under the other three role categories, list that value under 'Other' and notate that other life role. If you do not want to devote time and energy to a value, write that value under the 'Limited or No Expression' category.

Work/Academics	Important Relationships	Leisure/Community Activities
_____	_____	_____
_____	_____	_____
_____	_____	_____
_____	_____	_____
_____	_____	_____
_____	_____	_____
_____	_____	_____

Other	Limited or No Expression
_____	_____
_____	_____
_____	_____
_____	_____
_____	_____
_____	_____

INDEX

For Product Safety Concerns and Information please contact our EU
representative GPSR@taylorandfrancis.com
Taylor & Francis Verlag GmbH, Kaufingerstraße 24, 80331 München, Germany

www.ingramcontent.com/pod-product-compliance
Lightning Source LLC
Chambersburg PA
CBHW061253220326
41599CB00028B/5631

9 781032 208893